ODYSSEY
OF AN ELDER

Around the World in Eighty Days

GEORGE JERJIAN

Hasmark
PUBLISHING
INTERNATIONAL

Published by
Hasmark Publishing International
www.hasmarkpublishing.com

Copyright © 2025 George Jerjian
First Edition

All Rights Reserved.

No part of this book may be reproduced or transmitted in any form or by any means, electronic or mechanical, including photocopying, recording or by any information storage and retrieval system, without written permission from the author, except for the inclusion of brief quotations in a review.

Disclaimer

This book is designed to provide information and motivation to our readers. It is sold with the understanding that the publisher is not engaged to render any type of psychological, legal, or any other kind of professional advice. The content of each article is the sole expression and opinion of its author, and not necessarily that of the publisher. No warranties or guarantees are expressed or implied by the publisher's choice to include any of the content in this volume. Neither the publisher nor the individual author(s) shall be liable for any physical, psychological, emotional, financial, or commercial damages, including, but not limited to, special, incidental, consequential or other damages. Our views and rights are the same: You are responsible for your own choices, actions, and results.

Permission should be addressed in writing to George Jerjian at george@georgejerjian.com

Editor: Brad Green [brad@hasmarkpublishing.com]
Cover Design: Anne Karklins anne@hasmarkpublishing.com
Interior Layout: Amit Dey amit@hasmarkpublishing.com

ISBN 13: 978-1-77482-343-9
ISBN 10: 1-77482-343-8

Dedicated to all retirees who dare to seek a new beginning.

"Travel is fatal to prejudice, bigotry, and narrow-mindedness, and many of our people need it sorely on these accounts. Broad, wholesome, charitable views of men and things cannot be acquired by vegetating in one little corner of the earth all one's lifetime."

Mark Twain

"One of the great things about travel is that you find out how many good, kind people there are."

Edith Wharton

"Maybe the journey isn't about becoming anything. Maybe it's about unbecoming everything that isn't really you, so that you can be who you were meant to be in the first place."

Paulo Coelho

CONTENTS

Introduction xiii

PART 1 – South Africa 1
    Chapter 1   Cape Town 3
    Chapter 2   The Garden Route 7
    Chapter 3   Timbavati Nature Reserve 17

PART 2 – Australia 25
    Chapter 4   Sydney 27
    Chapter 5   Hamilton Island, Great Barrier Reef ... 35
    Chapter 6   Melbourne 47

PART 3 – New Zealand 63
    Chapter 7   Auckland 65
    Chapter 8   Coromandel Peninsula 69
    Chapter 9   Nelson 75
    Chapter 10   Kaikoura 81
    Chapter 11   Christchurch 85
    Chapter 12   Queenstown 91

PART 4 – Japan **97**
    Chapter 13 Tokyo........................... 99
    Chapter 14 Tsumago 107
    Chapter 15 Kanazawa....................... 113
    Chapter 16 Osaka........................... 121
    Chapter 17 Hiroshima & Miyajima............ 125
    Chapter 18 Kyoto........................... 133
    Chapter 19 Mount Koya 141
    Chapter 20 Osaka........................... 151
    Chapter 21 Mount Fuji 157
    Chapter 22 Tokyo........................... 165

PART 5 – Canada................................**169**
    Chapter 23 Vancouver, British Columbia......... 171
    Chapter 24 VIA Rail: The Canadian 175
    Chapter 25 Jasper, Alberta 181
    Chapter 26 Lake Louise, Alberta 187
    Chapter 27 Quebec City, Quebec............... 193
    Chapter 28 Lake Memphremagog, Quebec...... 205
Conclusion 209
Acknowledgments................................ 223
About the Author 227
Advance Praise 229

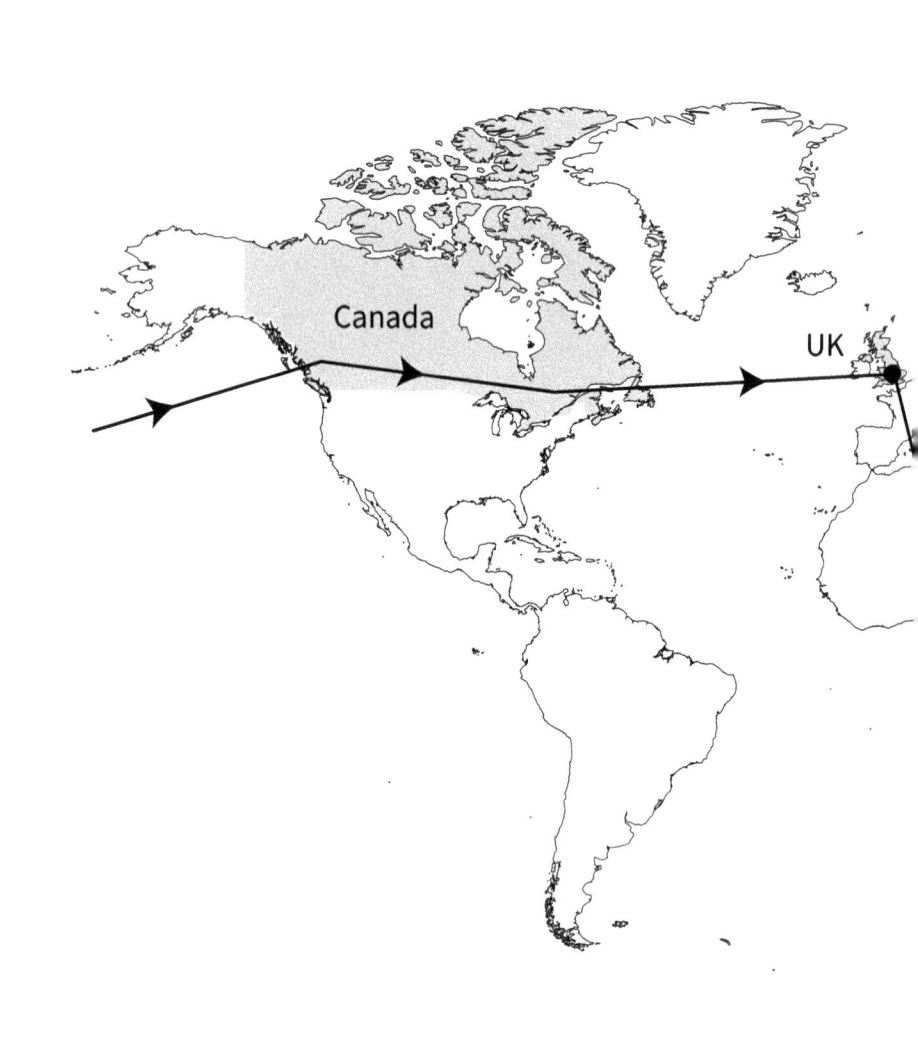

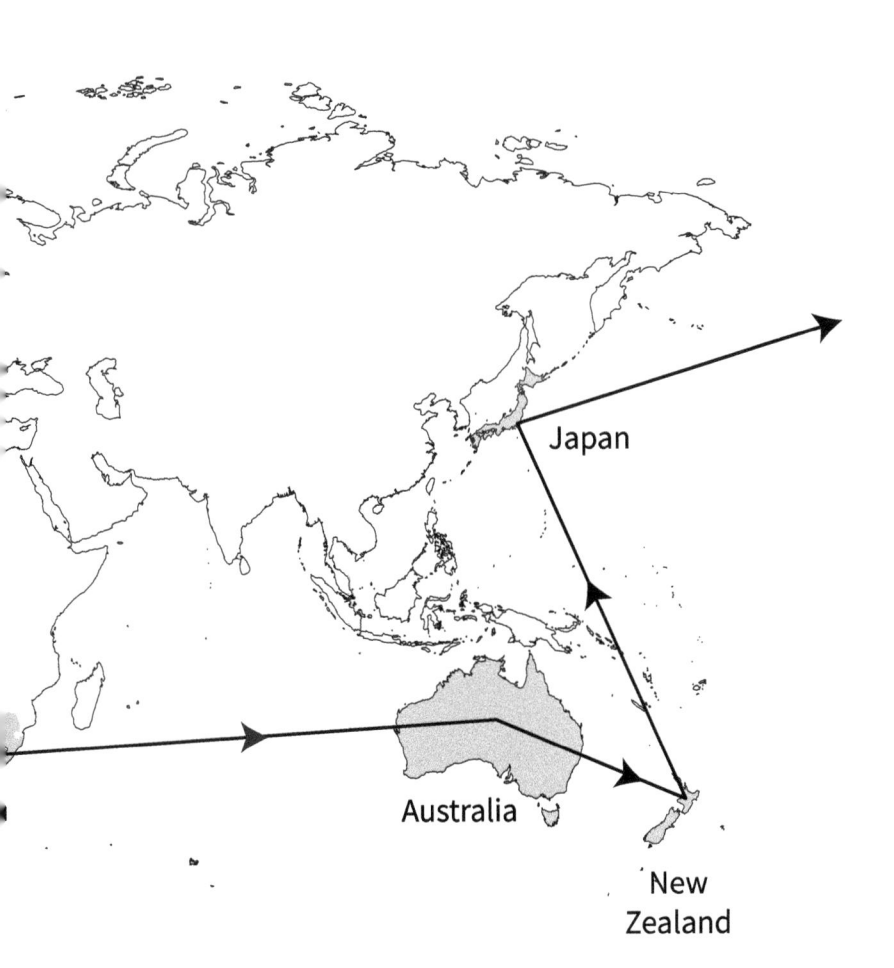

INTRODUCTION

In 2007, at the age of 52, I was diagnosed with a bone tumor and given six months to live. Thankfully, after three weeks, I discovered that the diagnosis was wrong, but I had to undergo two operations to remove the tumor. Over the following six months, I relearned how to walk. I semi-retired for almost 10 years. After a honeymoon period, I became unhappy and disillusioned with my retirement. In 2016, I went on a 30-day silent retreat, which I narrated in my book *Spirit of Gratitude: Crises are Opportunities* (2018). Thereafter, I became intrigued by mindset change, so I worked for 18 months with the late Canadian mindset coach Bob Proctor.

My work as a mindset mentor to retirees, which I started in 2017, not only transformed my life, but continues to do so. This book came about because I had recently been advising my clients to take a gap year after retiring. Yet, I had to admit to myself that I had not taken a gap year either—so how could I advise clients to do what I had not done? I had to walk my talk. In life, we are either growing or dying. If we are to continue growing, we must continue learning.

In December 2022, my wife and friend of 40 years agreed to divorce, and our divorce was granted a year later. While it was amicable, it was still very painful for both of us. With a

Catholic upbringing, divorce was a huge challenge. Obviously, she was not the person I had married—nor was I. That said, we had both evolved many times over and had made great efforts to navigate our marriage over the years. However, over the previous seven years, we had drifted apart. I describe it as our marriage wrapper tearing, making it unsustainable. Yet, our 40 years of friendship and our role as parents to two wonderful daughters could not be discarded; we had to continue nurturing it. We disagreed in a few important areas, like finances, but we did agree in crucial areas like love and trust. At this juncture in life, I needed space to find my new path.

It was then that I considered taking a gap year and making it an epic adventure—initially for myself, and then as a teaching tool for my clients. I chose to make this a personal journey above all, so I decided not to post on social media, allowing me to focus on my internal journey. As Mark Twain aptly put it, travel and education go hand in hand: "Travel is fatal to prejudice, bigotry, and narrow-mindedness." And to use Paulo Coelho's words, it is essential to "unbecome" everything that is not us, allowing our true selves to emerge.

Over months of contemplating the idea of a gap year, one thought kept resurfacing, and I kept dismissing it. Since adolescence, I had been captivated by French novelist Jules Verne's *Around the World in Eighty Days* and had always imagined embarking on a similar journey myself. Fast forward to 2023, and I continued dismissing it as a childish idea. Traveling the world for 80 days seemed costly in time, money, and effort. How would I benefit financially from it? Yet, the universe had my back. It kept dropping hints until I finally understood and relented.

The first hint was subtle. When I was looking to join a club in London, I revisited my old club, The East India Club in St. James's Square, which I had joined 30 years ago but left after 10 years. The club remained old-fashioned, maintaining its status as a gentlemen's club (no women allowed). I explored several other clubs and ultimately chose the Reform Club on Pall Mall—because I was in the reform business, it included women, its chair was a woman, and its ethos and history resonated with me. I became a member in 2022, and within a few months, I was reminded of the club's connection to Jules Verne and *Around the World in Eighty Days*. There was a temporary exhibition dedicated to the author and his book, and I attended a black-tie dinner with 150 members and guests celebrating the novel's 150th anniversary. For those unfamiliar, the story of *Around the World in Eighty Days* begins and ends at the club, where protagonist Phileas Fogg, a club member, wagers £20,000 (worth £500,000 today) that he can circumnavigate the world in 80 days. At the dinner, a professor of French literature regaled us with little-known facts about the author and the book. It was truly one of the most magical evenings I have had at the club.

The second hint came in Santa Fe, New Mexico, in May 2023, when I attended a reunion at Modern Elder Academy and stayed on for a balloon flight over the desert. As the balloon cruised downwind over the arid terrain, I asked the pilot what had led him to this profession. He told me that as a teenager, he had read *Around the World in Eighty Days* and was so captivated that he built his own balloon as a school project. He had worked with balloons his entire life, often in films, and shared tales of his escapades—including bribing his way out of jail in Egypt.

The third hint was more of a feeling. When I began researching potential destinations, I selected countries I had never visited before. I calculated costs for flights and accommodations to gauge the financial scope of the venture. The deeper I delved into planning, the more excited I became. I noticed how my spirit soared when I engaged in this process. This was how I wanted to feel every day—energized, excited, and enthusiastic. No more making myself small. No more avoiding things I wanted to do because of cost. I have one life, and I intend to live it fully. Strangely, this feeling resonated deeply with my body. *The Body Keeps the Score*, a book by psychologist Bessel van der Kolk, articulates how overwhelming experiences shape the brain, mind, and body awareness. In essence, if you're unhappy, it's because you're not doing what you should be doing—you're living someone else's script.

The fourth hint was the most striking. As I've explained, I had trouble convincing myself to spend this kind of money. At 69 years of age, newly separated from my wife and half of my savings, spending a substantial sum on an extravagant journey was daunting. I tried convincing myself that this money wasn't being wasted—that it was an investment in my future. But I needed more reassurance. With visits to five unfamiliar countries in 80 days, I enlisted Audley Travel, a leading UK boutique travel agency, to help plan my itinerary. Their country specialists helped me select the must-see locations and experiences while eliminating non-essentials. When Audley Travel presented the total cost of £39,650 ($49,652), my jaw dropped. Then it struck me—I actually had this money in my savings. In 2018, I had sold my share in a US real estate investment and had overpaid my taxes by $51,725 (£41,380). Despite my persistent follow-ups, the IRS delayed my refund for over three and a half years. The universe had kept this money untouched, and the IRS even paid an additional $6,112 in interest. It became clear: the universe had my back. A friend jokingly corrected me, saying, "George, the IRS *is* the universe!"

And so, it was planned. My trip would take me to five countries I had never visited: South Africa, Australia, New Zealand, Japan, and Canada (though I had previously visited Toronto several times to see my brother Simon and his family and attend Bob Proctor's training). I planned to spend two weeks in each country, except for Japan, where I would stay for three weeks. I secured travel and medical insurance for the 80-day journey and obtained the necessary electronic travel authorizations for Australia, New Zealand, and Canada. South Africa and Japan did not require visas. My departure from London was set for March 21, with my return scheduled for June 10, 2024. I was so prepared that I felt like I was walking on water.

PART 1

SOUTH AFRICA

"Africa changes you forever, like nowhere on earth. Once you have been there, you will never be the same."

Brian Jackman
Travel & Wildlife Writer

South Africa

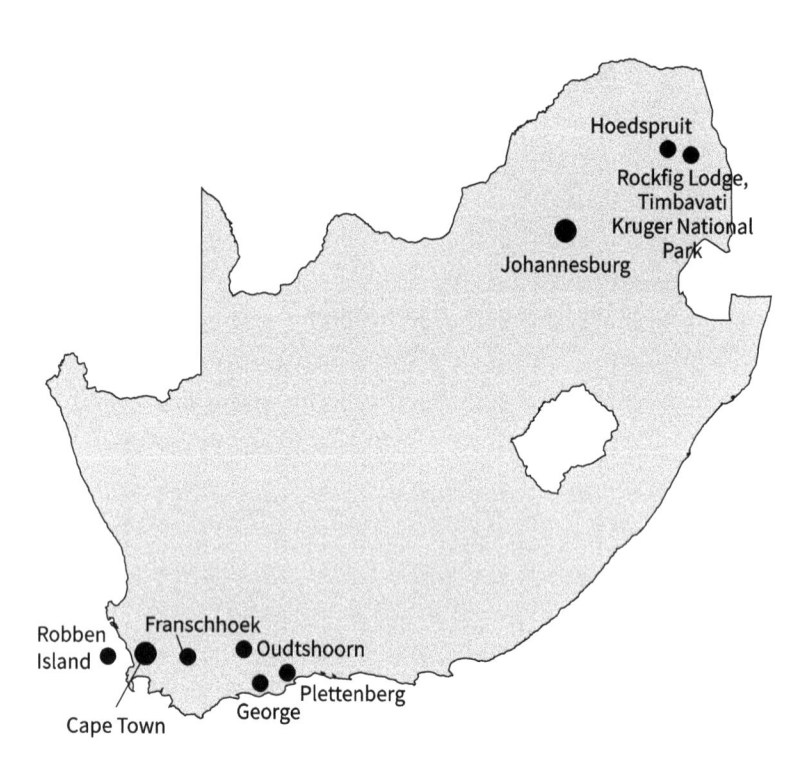

CHAPTER 1

Cape Town
21st – 24th March

My 12-hour British Airways flight from London landed in Cape Town the following day, Friday, March 22, at 8:00 a.m. My private taxi transfer took me directly to my hotel, the Victoria & Alfred Hotel on the waterfront. I arrived at the hotel reception just after 9:00 a.m. but discovered that my room would not be available until 3:00 p.m. I dropped my luggage at the front desk and waited in the lobby for my South African business partners to pick me up and take me to deliver a presentation to a dozen potential clients in the financial services industry.

Christi, a former barrister, picked me up, while his partner, Johan, a former pensions consultant, was organizing the equipment for my presentation. About half an hour later, Christi pulled into the parking lot of the Protea Hotel. Still in the clothes I had worn on the flight, I desperately needed to freshen up. I went to the bathroom, washed my face and neck, and ran water through my hair. Feeling energized, I ordered two double espressos to ensure I had the stamina for my one-hour presentation at 11:00 a.m. I entered the conference room with Christi and was introduced to four people present, while about six others watched online on a large screen.

The presentation went well, followed by an unexpectedly long hour of Q&A. At 2:00 p.m., Johan and Christi took me to lunch at a place called Jean's Winery. I chose a salad with kudu carpaccio—it was my first time tasting kudu, a large woodland antelope. It had a slightly gamey taste, but it was delicious. After returning to the hotel, I rested for a while. At 7:00 p.m., I went down to have dinner at a nearby restaurant called Quay 4, where I sat near the waterfront. I ordered grilled local fish, a good local red wine, and a crème brûlée. I was astonished at the bill. I thought I had miscalculated the exchange rate, but I hadn't—the bill was a quarter of what I would have paid in London. Pleased, I left my server a generous tip. By 8:30 p.m., I had crashed out.

Cape Town (population: 4,770,313) is South Africa's legislative capital. It is the country's oldest city and the seat of the Parliament of South Africa. It is also the second-largest city after Johannesburg. Nestled between Table Mountain and the ocean, it is a jewel of a city.

I woke early on Saturday, March 23, enjoyed breakfast, and walked to the Robben Island ferry pickup, scheduled to depart at 11:00 a.m. I was informed that all visits for the day had been canceled due to the buses on the island not working, so I rescheduled my visit for the following week. I took a taxi to the Belmond Mount Nelson Hotel, a sister hotel to the Belmond Cadogan Hotel in London. After admiring the elegant interior, I walked around its beautiful gardens. The guests all looked well-heeled. I had lunch on the veranda, feeling transported to colonial times—to what my birthplace, Khartoum, might have looked and felt like in the 1950s. I enjoyed tandoori chicken with naan bread, a side salad with yogurt, and a Castle Lite, a South African lager.

By 3:00 p.m., I was back at my hotel, where I met Christi and Johan. They took me to a nearby pub for a local lager and live music. Ninety minutes later, we walked to the local stadium to watch a rugby match, which kicked off at 5:00 p.m. The local team, the Stormers, were playing against Edinburgh. Seated in the front row near one end of the pitch, we were immediately drawn into the game. It was brilliant and riveting! The Stormers pulled no punches. They didn't play it safe; they attacked relentlessly. While Edinburgh put up a fight, the Stormers triumphed, winning 43–21.

On Sunday, March 24, Johan and his wife, Adri, picked me up from my hotel at 8:00 a.m. They took me on a personalized tour of Cape Town, including Signal Hill and the seaside promenade. Johan parked on a side street, and we entered Café Mantra, where we went upstairs to enjoy a marvelous breakfast with an ocean view.

CHAPTER 2

The Garden Route
24th – 26th March

That afternoon, I took a taxi to the airport for a domestic flight to the town of George (population: 157,394), which lies over 430 kilometers east of Cape Town along the famous Garden Route—a drive that can take up to five hours. After an hour in the air, my Airlink commuter plane landed in George. I walked toward the car rental desk at Avis, where two women were assisting customers. The process took some time because their computer systems were down. I finally managed to get a car—a white Nissan Almera—and drove for an hour and a quarter to reach Laird's Lodge, my accommodation near Plettenberg (population: 31,804), which is to South Africa what the Hamptons are to New York: a beautiful location and a playground for the wealthy.

National Geographic calls the Garden Route "the ultimate road trip," with its combination of world-class beaches, iridescent lagoons, and indigenous forests interspersed with welcoming towns such as Mossel Bay, George, Knysna, Wilderness National Park, Plettenberg Bay, and Storms River.

The next morning, after a sumptuous breakfast of two fried eggs, bacon, brown toast, and coffee, I drove to Robberg Marine Sanctuary, about 20 kilometers from Laird's Lodge. In the parking lot, a large, colorful board displayed three available trails. I chose the second option, the Witsand Circuit, a 5.5-kilometer hike with an estimated time of two hours. The trail led along the northern ridge of the peninsula. I was captivated by the crashing waves against the rocks below and the panoramic view of Plettenberg Beach behind me. The hiking path felt more like an obstacle course. Thankfully, I had brought my walking stick—the same one I had used to learn to walk again in 2007 after my bone tumor operation. I lost my balance at least a dozen times as I carefully placed my feet among the rocks ahead. My right leg has been weaker since the operation, and without my stick, I'm not sure I would have made it. I kid you not—a few times, I fell, cursed, and got up again! The path then veered right, away from the cliff edge, into a dense bush with a sandy trail that appeared to cross the peninsula. After about 10 minutes, I reached a sand dune.

In the distance to my right, I saw what looked like an island with the ocean on both sides. I turned right and walked down the long sand dune, all the way to the ocean. Turning right again, my feet sank into the sand with each step, making it an exhausting walk. I was panting and sweating. After about 15 minutes, I saw a sign indicating I should walk up to the rocks. I was exchanging a challenging sandy path for an equally challenging rocky one—the very definition of an obstacle course. I climbed the rocky path, which rose gradually but was even more perilous. I had been taking sips of water throughout the hike, but now my thirst was acute, my clothes were soaked with sweat, and I was more than ready for this hike to end. However, I still had to tackle one last challenge—climbing steep rocks before reaching the final stretch to the car park. When I finally arrived, I headed straight to the restroom, then to the canteen to buy an ice-cold bottle of water. As I drank and poured some over my head, I felt a small sense of accomplishment.

After breakfast the next day, I checked out of Laird's Lodge and drove to Knysna for coffee at East Head Café, which had been highly recommended at the hotel bar the night before. Then I drove to Wilderness (both the name of a town and a national park), about a 40-minute drive, to a place called Salinas Beach Restaurant, where I met Christi, who has a summer home nearby. We enjoyed a salad lunch before I set off again.

Oudtshoorn
26th – 27th March 2024

Back in the car, I drove north on the N12 to Oudtshoorn (population: 61,507), about 75 kilometers away—a drive of roughly 90 minutes. Halfway there, I was desperate to empty my bladder. There was nowhere to stop and no bush to hide behind. I was tempted to use an empty plastic bottle, but the risk of overspill made me reconsider, so I kept driving. A few miles later, I spotted a restaurant and stopped.

As I approached La Plume Hotel, I saw a platoon of ostriches within an enclosure. As my car neared, they ran away in formation. I checked in at La Plume, and while they prepared my room, I went for a massage to soothe my fatigued legs after yesterday's two-hour hike. Afterward, I sat on the veranda in a white-painted chair and journaled at a matching table, overlooking what, just for an instant, I imagined could have been my own personal estate, bordered by pink bougainvillea bushes around the hotel's perimeter.

At dinner, instead of playing it safe, I ordered an ostrich steak, served with potatoes and vegetables. I was a little nervous about how the meat would taste and whether I would even like it, but as it turned out, it was fabulous! If I hadn't been told it was ostrich, I wouldn't have known the difference between it and a fillet steak. Of course, the preparation played a key role. When I later asked the chef, she explained that she tenderizes it overnight and marinates it with butter and wine—no wonder it was so tender and juicy. If I had attempted to prepare it myself, it would undoubtedly have been inedible.

On Wednesday, March 27, at 8:00 a.m., I met with the paterfamilias of the Du Toit family, fourth-generation ostrich farmers whose origins trace back to Lille, France, and later to Franschhoek, the wine region of South Africa. Mr. Du Toit taught me a lot about ostriches. The black-feathered ones are male, while the grey-feathered ones are female. A female can hold between 12 and 22 eggs and lay them one after the other. To minimize risk, Du Toit uses incubation for the eggs. Female ostriches can produce eggs up to eight times a year for 20 years. Originally, ostriches were farmed for their feathers, which were fashionable for women's hats in the 18th and 19th centuries. Today, every part of the ostrich is utilized: its feathers, its skin for leather (Hermès Paris, for example, uses ostrich leather for its bags), its meat for steak, and everything else is processed into high-end pet food, especially for cats and dogs.

Franschhoek
27th – 28th March

That afternoon, I left ostrich country and headed for Franschhoek (population: 1,066), a 500-kilometer drive that would take about six hours. I drove through arid landscapes along the

R62, passing through Calitzdorp, Ladysmith, Barrydale, Montagu, and Ashton. Then I continued on the R60 from Robertson to Worcester, followed by the R42 to Villiersdorp. Finally, I took the R45, crossing the Three Waters Kloof and navigating endless mountain circuits before descending into the scenic landscape of Franschhoek.

After checking in at La Cabrière, which, with its white buildings and lavender gardens, looked more like a private plantation home, I ventured into town for dinner on the main street at Café Du Vin. For starters, I had a bobotie spring roll with minced meat, paired with a Simon 2022. My main course was a delicious Cape Malay chicken curry with yogurt and salsa, accompanied by a 2019 Merlot. For dessert, I enjoyed a lemon panna cotta with slices of mango, followed by a Boplaas 2018 Cape Vintage Reserve—another name for port.

On Thursday morning, after breakfast, I sat on the veranda outside my room at La Cabrière, gazing at the blue water of the swimming pool. It would have been inviting if not for the wind. I listened to the wind swaying the trees and rustling the swath of lavender planted outside my room. Wind has always symbolized the spirit—so what was the spirit telling me today? As I watched nature's splendor, I felt a deep desire to be close to it. Battersea Park in London just doesn't do it for me anymore. I deserve to be happy, and I sensed that spirit was urging me to prioritize my own happiness before I could help anyone else. I realized that I was discovering myself through this trip. For instance, I was able to complete the two-and-a-half-hour hike on Robberg Peninsula—exhausting yet exhilarating. However, I had been unable to find time for the Tsitsikamma Forest, which normally would have upset me. Fear of missing out, no doubt! In the past, I would have pushed on no matter what, just to tick that box. This time, I let it go—I didn't blame myself. I was kind to myself. The same thing happened in Oudtshoorn: I managed to visit the ostrich farm but skipped the Cango Caves Heritage Tour because adding two more hours to my already long six-hour drive would have been too much. No blame, no shame—I was good!

That morning, I walked into Franschhoek (which means "French corner" in Afrikaans). When King Louis XIV banned Protestantism in France in 1685, the French Huguenots fled to escape persecution. Around 300 of them arrived at the Cape of Good Hope in 1688 by ship and were given the Franschhoek Valley to settle.

I walked to the other end of town, where a bus station serves the wine trams that cover 45 wine farms. I purchased a ticket for the trams and selected two wineries to visit: Babylonstoren and Boschendal.

Babylonstoren took my breath away. The entire winemaking operation was housed in red brick buildings with stainless steel equipment. A museum explained every aspect of winemaking, from bottling to corking. The wine-tasting experience was unlike any I had ever had. The restaurant, a steel-framed structure with glass walls, showcased a panoramic view of the mountains in the background and vineyards in the foreground. At the center of the restaurant was a bar, with tables arranged around it. I sat near the window and enjoyed a large plate of salad, surrounded by various cold meats, cheeses, and breads, finished with a large yellow flower on the side of the plate. Fortified by this food, I was able to sample up to 10 different wines—white, rosé, and red—including their exquisite Mourvèdre Rosé, the official rosé wine of the RHS Chelsea Flower Show 2023.

Several hours later, I arrived at Boschendal Winery, where I indulged in a dessert pairing of five different wines of all colors, each accompanied by a different type of chocolate. It was an amazing day of exploration.

That evening, after having pizza for dinner in Franschhoek, it was still light, so I decided to walk back to the hotel to digest my meal. I had a nagging feeling to be cautious—walking alone on a road in South Africa is generally not recommended. I carried a pouch hanging from my neck containing my passport, some cash, credit cards, and my phone. Several cars passed, packed with passengers. If any one of them had stopped, they could easily have overpowered me and taken my belongings. The thought unsettled me. Lost in these worries, I suddenly realized I had walked too far—I didn't know where I was. Google Maps was no help. I spotted a business premises with a driveway nearby, so I stopped and pretended to be talking on the phone in case anyone was watching. Then I called the local taxi service I had used earlier. A cab arrived in 10 minutes, but those 10 minutes felt like an eternity.

Cape Town
29th - 31st March

I left Franschhoek after breakfast, bidding farewell to my wonderful host, Lisa. The drive to Cape Town took 90 minutes. Upon arrival at Welgelegen—quite the tongue twister—my new hotel, my room was not yet ready. The hotel manager, an attractive young South African woman named Memory (a name one doesn't easily forget), promised to look after my bags. I took a taxi to Table Mountain, aiming to arrive by 10:20 a.m. When I reached the entrance, I realized I had left my ticket in my suitcase and had to purchase a new one. The line for the cable car was slow-moving, taking 80 minutes. Once at the top, I stayed for 30 minutes, taking in the panoramic views of

Cape Town, before descending just after noon and catching a taxi back to my hotel to meet my old Toastmaster friend, Bill Russell. Bill drove us to the waterfront, parked in a lot, and we walked to Harbour House Restaurant, where his wife, Jeri, was already seated at a table facing the water. We had a wonderful meal and conversation. I ordered local grilled clipfish with risotto, vegetables, and a glass of South African Chardonnay.

On Saturday morning, after breakfast, I took a taxi to the V&A Waterfront to visit Robben Island. As we lined up to board the catamaran, my eyes landed on a quote by Nelson Mandela, etched on a wall: "It is said that no one truly knows a nation until one has been inside its jails." I reflected on the profound truth of that statement. After 40 minutes at sea, the catamaran arrived at Robben Island harbor. The ominous, angular concrete slab walls foreshadowed the hardship within. We boarded a bus, and the tour guide delivered a loud, emotionally charged talk on the history and geography of the island and its buildings, almost as if it were a guilt-inducing performance.

Our guide for the next part of the prison tour was a former political prisoner who had been incarcerated there at the age of 21 for sabotage and remained for more than a decade. I was struck by his humility, gentleness, and kindness.

He showed us a large communal cell where he and about 60 others had been confined together. They had showers and toilet facilities but slept on mats with blankets. Mandela and the other intellectuals in Block B had small single cells with only a mat, a blanket, and a red bucket for sanitation—no toilets or showers. We saw the yard in Block B where Mandela and his fellow prisoners spent their leisure time and the tree under which he had hidden his manuscript, as recounted in his memoir.

During the Q&A, I asked the guide what their diet consisted of. He replied, "Mainly porridge and maize meal, with black bread occasionally." When I inquired whether he had ever been beaten or tortured, he hesitated, his voice catching as he said, "You're taking me to a dark place." He then shared a story: while working in the limestone quarry, a young inmate lit a cigarette without permission. The guards, enraged, prepared to beat him. The guide and a few others raised their shovels to protect the novice. In retaliation, the guards set their German Shepherds on them, and he was hospitalized for two weeks.

As we prepared to leave Robben Island, I asked our guide for his name. He replied with a wry smile, "You're not going to report me, are you?" I reassured him, "Of course not, I just want to honor you in my book." He told me his name—Vuliani. I took a photograph with him before walking the long march back to the boat.

On Safari in the Timbavati Private Nature Reserve with Rockfig Safari Lodge's driver and guide, Lorence, and Fumani, tracker

CHAPTER 3

Rockfig Lodge, Timbavati Nature Reserve
31st March – 5th April

The Airlink commuter flight landed at East Gate Airport, the gateway to the Timbavati Private Nature Reserve (spanning over 500 square kilometers) and adjacent to the much larger Kruger National Park (almost 20,000 square kilometers). East Gate Airport was a single small building, hidden behind trees and foliage. Only one other aircraft was parked on the tarmac. I felt transported back to the Africa of my childhood—to what was once the wonderful country of Sudan. To be honest, even Khartoum Airport was significantly larger and more technologically advanced. Here at East Gate, there were no conveyor belts; luggage was delivered hand to hand. As I waited for my bags, a man approached me holding a piece of white paper with my name on it. Soon, we were on the road to Rockfig, my lodge in the Timbavati, closer to Mozambique than to Johannesburg.

As we arrived at Rockfig, the place looked heavenly and pristine. Three female staff members stood at the entrance to welcome me. Their warmth, politeness, and hospitality made me feel like a VIP or even a celebrity. Lunch was chicken skewers on a bed of pita and hummus, topped with salad. An hour after settling into my room, I was already on my first afternoon safari—no slacking here. Our vehicle, a Toyota Land Cruiser customized for safaris, was manned by Lorence, our driver and guide, and Fumani, our tracker. Accompanying us were an English mother and daughter. On this first drive, I saw an elephant crossing our path, a troop of impalas, a warthog eating from a bush, a startled giraffe staring at us, a zebra munching grass, several other zebras with their young, a solitary wildebeest, and, finally, the showpiece—a pride of lions.

At first, I didn't spot the lions. Lorence pointed them out, lying in the savanna, camouflaged and enjoying their siesta. Then, slowly, two young males lifted their heads and wandered off while the others stayed put. We noticed three cubs. For the next hour, we followed the pride as they stalked some zebras for that evening's hunt. The zebras yelped in alarm, and the lions failed in their pursuit. With Fumani manning the searchlight, we tracked a lioness into the night. Her three cubs wanted to join in, but one deadly stare from their mother made them whimper and stay low. Now in complete darkness, Lorence drove us back to the lodge. I relished the chill evening breeze and the star-studded sky, with Orion pointing the wrong way in the southern hemisphere. It felt incredible to be alive in this moment!

On Monday, I was up at 5:15 a.m. for my first morning safari. At the meeting point, I was offered a mug of black coffee and a corn muffin before we set off. I was the only passenger for Lorence and Fumani, and I didn't realize at the time that I would remain their sole guest for the next three days. Soon, I witnessed a glorious African sunrise—hues of orange and yellow piercing through the blue sky and stretching across the lush green landscape. I felt immense joy breathing in the clean, crisp air.

Lorence drove for 45 minutes. We saw an impala with its offspring, a zebra, an eagle perched on a marula tree, and a giraffe nibbling leaves high up in the branches. Then, we stumbled upon a lion sleeping in the savanna, its stomach heaving heavily, its face strained with discomfort, and its mouth stained red with blood. "The kill must be nearby," Lorence said. He turned the vehicle around a nearby tree, and there it was—a dead wildebeest, its belly torn open, scarlet red, its horns caught in the lower branches.

The listless lion suddenly stirred and walked toward its kill, as if ensuring we wouldn't steal its meal. We observed closely. It attempted several times to drag the carcass away from the tree but failed. Eventually, it settled down, found a comfortable position, and resumed gorging, occasionally turning to glance at us with bloodied mouth and paws. After half an hour, we returned to the lodge for a well-earned breakfast.

At 4:00 p.m., we set off again in the Land Cruiser in search of whatever awaited us that afternoon. We encountered a group of warthogs, a large and a small rhinoceros, a Nyala tree, and a pack of wild dogs—ugly and smelly, their sand-colored skin marked with black and white patches, their large ears twitching like antennae. Suddenly, the entire pack began chasing a lone impala. We pursued them at full speed but lost sight of them. Later, on our way back to the lodge, we crossed paths with another safari vehicle from a neighboring lodge. They told us they had seen a pack of dogs devouring an impala.

Nature is beautiful, but it is also cruel. Why are we surprised when humans are cruel?

On Tuesday, we set off at 6:00 a.m. as usual. The fresh, crisp air tingled on my skin and filled my nostrils. Soon, I witnessed another breathtaking African sunrise—a glowing orange sun spreading its rays across the blue sky. Today,

Lorence was hoping to show me a leopard and a buffalo. He was determined to help me complete my sightings of the Big Five (elephant, lion, leopard, buffalo, and rhinoceros) and the Ugly Five (hyena, vulture, warthog, wildebeest, and marabou stork). We drove at a steady pace along the dirt track through the savanna.

The radio crackled with the voice of Liam, the head guide at Rockfig, directing Lorence to the Rockfig airstrip. Lorence floored the accelerator. As we reached the end of the landing strip, we found more than a dozen wild dogs lounging about—but what were they waiting for? Within minutes, more than six vehicles arrived to witness this peculiar gathering.

We then moved on and soon spotted three hyenas. Their ugliness fascinated me, and the fear they inspired intrigued me. I wondered what it would be like to be a hyena or a wild dog for a day. Would I end up hating myself, or would I enjoy the camaraderie of hunting with a pack of like-minded killers? These animals are what they are—they do not pretend to be something else. In their world, they must kill to survive. In our human world, we rarely kill for food; we kill for power, passion, and possession.

Lorence continued driving until we encountered several rhinoceroses—two males, followed by a mother and her calf, who fled as soon as they saw us. At a watering hole, we spotted another pair drinking. As we carried on, we saw several giraffes, zebras, and impalas, then more zebras crossing the road. Lastly, we spotted a majestic kudu, one of the largest antelopes on the reserve, with half a dozen thin white stripes along its side. Lorence helped me identify numerous birds and trees unique to the region.

At 4:00 p.m., we set out again. For an hour, we saw the usual suspects—zebras, impalas, and giraffes sticking together as herbivores, wary of predators. Then, suddenly, a voice crackled over the radio. It was Liam. A leopard had been spotted. Lorence knew exactly where to go. He floored the gas pedal, and we sped along a rugged track through a dry riverbed—what he called an "African Massage"—until we reached a cluster of safari vehicles already at the scene. Even when we were just six meters away, I struggled to make out the leopard's outline until Fumani pointed it out in the tall grass ahead.

My heart pounded. We had spent days hoping to see a leopard, and here we were. The leopard's beauty and elegance made the lion seem almost ordinary. Unlike the lion, which thrives in a pride, the leopard is a solitary creature. It reminded me of a samurai—a lone warrior. Now I understood why the Zulu chief is adorned in leopard skin during ceremonies. In fact, Rockfig, the lodge where I was staying, was named after a beloved leopard owned by its South African proprietor, Bruce Jenkins.

That evening, I was late for pre-dinner drinks at the sundowner fire circle. By the time I arrived, all the guests were already seated around the fire, drinks in hand. A young, fair-haired English financier, sitting beside his wife and two kids, called out to me in a commanding voice, "George, regale us with a story."

"I just got here—let someone else start," I replied.

With a grin, he insisted, "Everyone's already done it. You're next."

This couple had irritated me for days with their sense of entitlement, and I had done my best to avoid them. But here I was, compelled to take the bull by the horns.

So, I stood up. My go-to accent for humor is a thick Russian one, which had won me a humorous speech competition at Toastmasters in London a decade ago. I looked directly at the Englishman, pointed my index finger at him, and in my best Russian accent, said, "Ve haf met bee-fore—in Kyev, at a naytclub 10 yers ago. I ree-member you. You were vith a blond vooman, but not ze one here vith you. I know all about your… sexual proclivities. You know khaw? Because zat vooman in Kyev—she vas my operative. Shall ve continue zis conversation in private?"

Everyone burst into laughter around the fire, including the Englishman and his wife. He came over and patted me on the back, in what felt like a king acknowledging his jester. I knew I had struck a chord. He didn't speak to me again that evening—or at any time after.

Wednesday, April 3, was my late father's birthday. Oh, how I miss him! I woke up at 5:15 a.m., and we set off just before 6:00. For the first 10 minutes, we saw nothing, until we spotted a baby grey duiker standing forlorn in the middle of the road. It looked like a baby fawn—so vulnerable and innocent.

Lorence said, "It must have lost its mother to a predator. No mother would leave her offspring unattended."

We gently guided it off the road. As we continued, Fumani noticed leopard tracks. Both Lorence and Fumani asked if they could step out of the car to track them. I agreed, and they went off on foot. Twenty minutes later, they returned and reported seeing signs that a leopard had dragged something heavy—possibly the mother of our lost duiker. We searched for another 20 minutes but found nothing, so we carried on down the dirt road.

Nature holds so many secrets and mysteries. My so-called civilized mind couldn't see what Lorence and Fumani could. Their minds were trained to decipher what was hidden. Mine assumed information was freely available—but clearly, it was not. In our world, truth is obscured, surrounded by misinformation and deception. To truly see, hear, and feel reality, we must learn to quiet our minds and hearts.

Thursday morning's drive was neither eventful nor uneventful. We saw the usual suspects. However, back at Rockfig for lunch, as I sat down with a ginger beer before my meal, a woman suddenly alerted us—a herd of elephants was approaching the watering hole just beyond the swimming pool. Guests and staff alike rushed out to watch. At least 15 elephants, ranging from massive adults to a newborn calf, drank deeply. A massive elephant—likely the matriarch—and several young ones splashed water over their backs.

In the afternoon, new guests joined us: Tracey and her 10-year-old son, Huxley. They were Americans of Taiwanese origin, living in the San Francisco Bay Area. On the drive, I helped Tracey identify specific birds and animals for her guidebook. The dynamic between Lorence, Fumani, and me shifted with their presence—but in a good way. We exchanged stories, shared knowledge, and bonded. That evening, after washing and changing, we met again at the sundowner fire site for drinks, followed by a 'Braai'—the South African barbecue. It was a great dinner with wonderful conversation. I went to bed early, as the next morning would be my last safari.

Friday's wake-up call was, as always, at 5:15 a.m. After coffee, a muffin, and a ginger biscuit, I filled my water bottle, and we made our way to the Land Cruiser. With Tracey, Huxley, Fumani, and myself on board, Lorence accelerated onto the dirt track. For the first hour, we enjoyed the sunrise and checked off new birds on our list. Then, we spotted the usual suspects—zebras, giraffes, and impalas—and a wild rabbit or two.

Then came the usual crackling over the radio—a leopard had been spotted.

Lorence immediately steered toward the location, navigating without road markings or compass. When we arrived, we saw the leopard lying in the grass, rubbing its head against the ground—perhaps to rid itself of lice or insects. Then it rolled over twice and began licking itself before finally standing up and walking away.

It was magical to see this elegant yet powerful creature one last time before I left this paradise. I had learned so much about nature here.

Back at the lodge, I had breakfast with Lorence, Tracey, and Huxley. Then, before boarding my waiting taxi, I hugged the guests and staff at Rockfig goodbye. As my taxi drove me to East Gate Airport for my flight to Johannesburg, I reflected on my time in Africa. This land touches something primal and visceral in a way no other place can.

Landing at Johannesburg Airport and transferring to my onward Qantas flight to Sydney, I felt light-hearted, unfazed by the fact that I was about to endure another 12-hour flight.

15 days completed.

65 days remaining.

PART 2

AUSTRALIA

"Don't worry about the world coming to
an end today.
It is already tomorrow in Australia."

Charles M Schulz (1922-2000)
American cartoonist

Australia

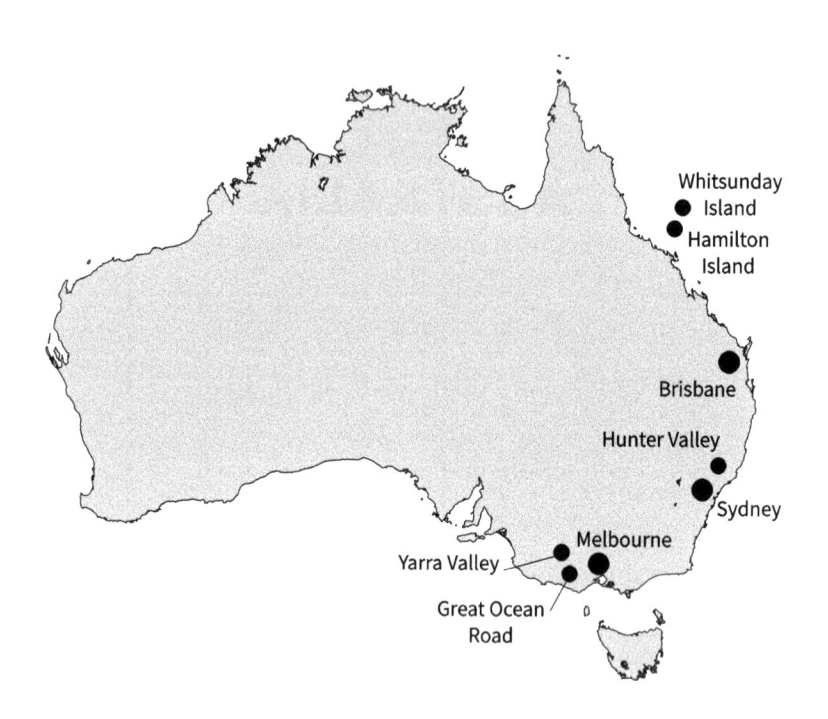

- Whitsunday Island
- Hamilton Island
- Brisbane
- Hunter Valley
- Sydney
- Yarra Valley
- Melbourne
- Great Ocean Road

CHAPTER 4

Sydney
5th – 10th April

The phone rang in my hotel room at 7:20 a.m. I was in a deep sleep, having only checked in a few hours earlier after enduring a 12-hour flight in a middle seat. I'm not complaining, just explaining the reality of my situation. On the other end of the line was my tour guide for a scheduled hike in the Blue Mountains, west of Sydney. I opened the curtain—it was still raining. The idea of trekking through mud didn't appeal to me, so I politely declined and went back to bed for a couple more hours.

After breakfast at 9:30 a.m. at my hotel, the Amora Jamieson, I walked about 30 minutes to the Australian Museum to explore the history of the First Nations and Australia's minerals. Two hours later, I took an immaculately clean and modern tram to Circular Quay to visit Sydney's iconic harbor and the Opera House. After an hour, I stopped for lunch at an outdoor restaurant, ordering a poke bowl with chicken and an Asahi lager. I then wandered central Sydney for another two hours, both to digest my food and to get a better sense of the city. On my way back, Google Maps let me down, and I got lost for a good hour before finally finding my hotel.

My first impressions of Sydney? It's more attractive than Toronto, primarily because of the weather. The urban area feels new, youthful, and vibrant, with an efficient and beautiful tram system—clean, fast, and a fraction of the cost of London transport. Sydney and Melbourne both have populations of just over five million.

Today is a special day on my calendar: my daughter Elizabeth's 31st birthday. I called her on WhatsApp, and we talked for a long while. Even though she's an independent adult, managing life just fine without me, she's still 5,000 miles away. As a father, I find myself worrying about her for no real reason. I suppose it's a good thing that she doesn't yet have to worry about me.

On Sunday morning at 9:30 a.m., I had arranged to meet Ang Galloway, a *campadre* from a week-long retreat at the Modern Elder Academy in Baja California Sur, Mexico, in 2022. We met at Pier 4 of Circular Quay. I hadn't expected a marathon walk, but with Ang, you do as she says. We embarked on a two-hour, fast-paced trek past the Opera House, through Farm Cove, into the Royal Botanic Gardens, and then back to Sydney Cove via The Rocks, an area under the Harbour Bridge. We returned to Circular Quay at 11:30 a.m. to go home, freshen up, and meet again at 12:50 p.m. for lunch with Alex, another friend from Baja.

Alex arrived in her Range Rover, picked us up, and drove us to Bondi Beach, where we dined at Icebergs, a restaurant perched over the crashing waves. I had an octopus salad to start, followed by grilled cod with olive and lemon, accompanied by two glasses of local Chardonnay. We reminisced about our time in Mexico, enjoying the view. Four hours later, Alex had to leave, so Ang's daughter drove us back to Circular Quay in her mother's Mercedes sports car.

Monday morning greeted me with beautiful sunshine. Skyscrapers surrounded me, but cities no longer hold the magic they once did. I miss the simple pleasures of nature, especially the African savanna. I must learn to be present wherever I am—even while drinking coffee. I had my morning coffee absentmindedly and immediately craved another, as if I hadn't had one at all.

Today, my heart pines for something deeper. I keep asking myself: Why am I unable to let go of this sinking feeling? What is holding me back, and why? Why can't I let go of this unease? Questions swirl in my head, but answers elude me. I am marinating in uncertainty. Still, I trust my heart to guide me. It will not lead me astray. For now, I must continue my path and let time take care of the rest. It always does.

I set off to find the Radisson Blu Hotel, a short walk from mine, where a minivan was waiting to take a group to Hunter Valley's wineries. Jeff, our guide and driver, directed me over the phone to the pickup point. I arrived 15 minutes late. The group—already seated—gave me disapproving looks. Jeff had me sit in the front seat beside him. I apologized for my tardiness and asked for their forbearance. The drive to Hunter Valley would take a few hours, so I struck up a conversation with Jeff.

A Scotsman from Glasgow, he had visited a friend in Australia 42 years ago and never left. We reminisced about British TV shows from the 1970s and '80s: *Rising Damp*, *Tommy Cooper*, *Up Pompeii!* with Frankie Howerd, and more.

After two and a half hours, we reached our first winery, Sadler's Creek. My fellow travelers, seated at two tables, included a family of three from New York, two older single women from Melbourne, and a man from Rhode Island—a former defense employee, an alpha male type whose wife sat at the other table. Our wine assistant was a scholarly-looking young man but lacked charm and charisma. We sampled half a dozen wines, but none made the earth shake.

The second winery, Hanging Tree, had a livelier atmosphere. Our host, a gregarious Aussie, introduced us to their sparkling wine, explaining that because it's illegal to use the word "prosecco" in Australia, they had adopted two alternatives: "Ozsecco" and "Proseccoroo." Everyone laughed. The wines were good, and two of the American women in the group got the giggles at my jokes. I discovered that two of the couples were siblings—a Chinese American brother and sister, traveling with their spouses. They were a delight. The sister-in-law, an introvert and keen observer, touched my arm at one point and said sincerely, "I wish you were coming with us on our cruise—you're such fun."

By now, we were all tippled and hungry. We boarded the minivan for lunch at our third stop, Cypress Lakes Golf Club. Our group had a reserved table in the club room. I ordered chicken Milanese with salad and a glass of Merlot.

After lunch, Jeff drove us to the Hunter Valley Cheese Factory, where we sampled five local cheeses, paired with biscuits and condiments. We then stopped briefly at a chocolate factory, where I bought a packet of chocolate-covered orange peels—one of my favorites. Our final stop was Ernest Hill, a small winery with fine wines, though none to my taste.

Back at my hotel by 6:00 p.m., exhausted, I scrolled through Instagram and stumbled upon a post. The message resonated: an invitation to listen to our inner wisdom. I must trust the divine message I received in Santa Fe, while hallucinating on magic mushrooms: "George, you are deeply, deeply loved." I have already set in motion my uprising against my acquired persona, the one causing me psychic pain and inner conflict. My faith will get me through this middle passage. With that I recalled James Hollis' words from his book *The Middle Passage* (1993):

> "I acknowledge the partiality of the lens given by my family, and culture, and things with which I made my choices, and suffered the consequences. The person who I was before is gone, yet the person I am to become has not materialized, so I am in a liminal space. The first must die and be grieved for. Such death is not an end, but a passage. This middle passage from the false self to authenticity."

I feel like the river in Khalil Gibran's poem *The River Cannot Go Back*:

> *The river cannot go back.*
> *Nobody can go back.*
> *To go back is impossible in existence.*
> *The river needs to take the risk*
> *of entering the ocean*
> *because only then will fear disappear,*
> *because that's where the river will know*
> *it's not about disappearing into the ocean,*
> *but of becoming the ocean.*

Tonight, as I sleep, I will flow into the ocean.

On Tuesday morning, I found myself on the 36th floor of the Shangri-La Hotel for breakfast with an old Aussie friend from London, Stephen Digby, a lawyer I had met over 20 years ago when he worked in London. He had long since settled back in Australia with his English wife. When he arrived, we discovered that the restaurant was fully booked, so we went down to find another venue. We walked to The Rocks and found breakfast at the Belgian Café. We each had a long black (as an Americano is known here) and our own version of eggs Benedict—mine with bacon, his with salmon. We talked about the possibility of me doing business in Australia, including a wild idea of top executives taking an "Around the World in Eighty Days" trip while completing my eight-week course. We parted ways near the Museum of Contemporary Art, where I noticed two ibises, followed by a flock grazing on a patch of long grass. I thought of my brother Chris and our days at Ibis Plaza, a commercial property in New Jersey that we had managed for 35 years.

I took a tram back to my hotel, changed into my shorts, went down to the lobby, and ordered an Uber. Twenty minutes later, I arrived at Bondi Beach to start my coastal walk. I set off on a path toward Icebergs restaurant, where I had lunched on Sunday with Ang and Alex. I continued along the coastal walk, past the rocks and crashing waves. Climbing up and down stairs, I passed Mackenzie's Point Lookout. Before reaching Tamarama Point, I spotted a striking woman with ginger hair in a ponytail, wearing sunglasses and holding a leash. I asked if I was on the right path to Coogee. She confirmed that I was and explained the route. A few dozen feet later, I stopped to take a photo, and she passed by again with her white poodle, offering more details. She told me she lived nearby and loved this place. I walked a few hundred yards and paused, wondering if she would stop again. She did. I wasn't sure what to make of it. Stop whatever you're thinking! Soon after, she said she had to get home, and I continued to Tamarama Beach on Mackenzie's Bay.

I walked on to Nelson Bay, where Bronte Beach is located. I saw a graceful woman in her seventies, panting and out of breath. I said to her, "I know how you feel." She touched my arm and said, "You're a good man." I wondered where all these compliments were coming from—maybe it was the energy I was exuding. I followed the coastal path past the lookout point into Waverley Cemetery. Reading the names and dates on the tombstones—mostly from the 18th century but some as recent as 2020—I felt grateful for my life and the wonder of this journey.

As I exited the cemetery, a young man with a strong French accent approached me and introduced himself as Ollie, a 25-year-old from Paris. As we walked, Ollie said he was on a special visa, spending 10 months traveling in Australia and working in French restaurants along the way. He shared an interesting fact: over 100,000 young French people come to Australia each year on his type of visa. His ambition was to open his own restaurant in Paris. Before that, he had worked in procurement at SNCF, the French national railway company. My brief encounter with this young Frenchman felt surreal, as if I were a character in *The Canterbury Tales*, and our conversation was part of a pilgrimage, like two travelers on the Camino de Santiago.

We continued our walk past Clovelly Beach, around Gordons Bay, past Koojah Cliff, and into Coogee. Swerving away from the beach, we stopped at Coogee Pavilion, a restaurant the ginger-haired woman had recommended. I was famished, so we stopped for a bite. I had pappardelle with sausage, which was delicious. As we walked to the bus stop, it started to rain. We boarded Bus 373 to the Museum, then took the subway two stops to Circular Quay, where we parted ways. By the time I got back to the hotel, the rain was coming down hard, and I was completely drenched.

Hiking to Coral Cove on Hamilton Island, Great Barrier Reef

CHAPTER 5

Hamilton Island, Great Barrier Reef
10th – 15th April

Very early on Wednesday morning, I boarded a nonstop, two-and-a-half-hour Qantas flight from Sydney Airport to Hamilton Island. To make the most of my limited time, I wanted to get as close to the Great Barrier Reef as possible without stopping in Brisbane, Cairns, or Port Douglas.

Hamilton Island is part of a group of 74 mostly uninhabited islands known as the Whitsundays. Located in the heart of the Great Barrier Reef, Hamilton Island, with a population of fewer than 1,500 people, is one of Australia's most spectacular and sought-after holiday destinations, surrounded by pristine white beaches and a kaleidoscope of coral and marine life. The island is car-free but full of white electric golf buggies, which rent for A$130 a day.

On the flight, I noticed that the skin on both my lower arms, which had turned chili red after my Robberg Peninsula hike in South Africa two weeks earlier, was now shedding like a snake's. The skin is the body's largest organ, with an intelligence much like a cell's membrane. I wondered if shedding my skin was somehow resonant with the changes in my life.

As the aircraft began its descent into Hamilton Island Airport, I looked out the window and saw the lush green landscape of the tropical island. Floating on the shimmering water of the marina were hundreds of white yachts and sailboats, neatly parked side by side. Even before landing, Hamilton Island seemed poised to rival St. Barth's and St. Tropez. After collecting our luggage, a minivan took us to the Reef View Hotel and Resort, where I was booked to stay for the next five days. As I waited in the lobby for my room to become available, I spent some time journaling.

After settling into my room, I went down to the beach opposite the Reef View Hotel—Catseye Beach—where the waters were calm in this sheltered bay. I sat on a lounger and gazed at the endless ocean for about 30 minutes before making my way back to my room to rest, shower, and journal my thoughts and activities for the day.

While scrolling on Instagram, I came across a post about the stages of detachment. The entire purpose of my trip was to detach from my past life so I could embark on a new one. The post caught my attention, so I decided to journal the stages of detachment for myself.

1. **Acknowledgement**: Deep within my emotions, I feel a longing for a profound, all-consuming idea—a worthy cause. I want to exist in this state constantly, to adore it and to be adored by it. My heart sinks when I lose faith in it.

2. **Self-inquiry**: This craving for love, adoration, and devotion is so powerful, so seductive—almost heavenly, almost impossible—but I know it is not. I observe myself in this devotion.

3. **Processing**: I have learned that it is impossible for a human to sustain this level of devotion indefinitely, just as it may be impossible for someone to endure being the object of such devotion all the time. It becomes a form of enslavement. Where can this energy go? How can I transform it?
4. **Creative action**: I seek new beginnings. I want to shift from merely processing to actively doing. With the insights and personal growth, I have gained so far, I now want to find a community of like-minded people who resonate with this emotion.
5. **Freedom**: The past no longer holds power over me. I have grieved long enough. Now, I must live. I release myself from attachments to desires, losses, and expected outcomes. This freedom allows me to exist in the present—happy, content, and with a deep knowing that the universe has my back and will provide something even greater than I can imagine.

I had made a note that dinner in the hotel started as early as 5:30 p.m., so I went down to have an early dinner to ensure I could also sleep early. The restaurant was already filling up with parents and their toddlers. For the first time, I did not feel alone. Nor did I long for the love and warmth of a family or a partner. I was content in my solitude, without the burden of caring for children or anyone else. I had done that for 40 years—I had paid my dues. Now, I needed to look after myself, to reinvent who I was and embrace the purpose that had found me. I was truly shedding my skin. Tonight, I would sleep with peace in my heart and mind. Tomorrow was another day.

On Thursday morning, I woke up at 6:00 a.m. and went downstairs for breakfast: two boiled eggs, two slices of brown bread with butter and honey, and a black coffee. By 7:30 a.m., I was on my way to the scenic trail entrance of Catseye Beach. I aimed to complete the walk to Coral Cove, about 2.3 kilometers one way—or 4.6 kilometers for the full return trip—taking around two hours.

As I approached the first section of the trail, it was wide but steep. My breathing grew heavy, and my legs ached already, making me question how difficult this trail might be. The path soon narrowed, and to my left was a steep canyon. After 30 minutes, I reached Saddle Junction, where various routes branched off. I chose the one leading to Coral Cove. Intermittently, between the trees, I glimpsed the ocean—a seductive sight, not unlike a woman wearing a skirt with a deep slit, revealing a flash of her leg with every step. The sound of waves lapping the shore put me at ease. The path ahead was strewn with rocks, stones, broken branches, and protruding tree roots. I had to remain alert, focusing on both my footing and my breath. Another 30 minutes later, I finally reached Coral Cove. It was picturesque, but for some reason, I had expected the sand to be a brilliant silica white.

Coral Cove lay on the opposite side of the island from Catseye Beach and the Reef View Hotel. By 8:30 a.m., I began my return journey. My bladder was full, so I took a few moments to mark my territory against a tree, much like our canine friends. Though it was technically winter here in the Southern Hemisphere, the heat had already settled in before 9:00 a.m.

An hour later, I made my way to the Tour Bookings Bureau to confirm that my tours on Friday the 12th and Sunday the 14th were still scheduled. While there, I also arranged a sunset cruise for 5:00 p.m. that evening and purchased an SPF-50 sunscreen lotion. Stopping for lunch at a café, I had a pasta salad and a glass of Coke, then ambled toward the beach for a swim in the ocean—without a wetsuit. I only stayed in the water for a delightful 15 minutes, wary of jellyfish.

At 5:00 p.m., I boarded the *Explorer* catamaran, and we set sail around the Whitsunday Islands. For an hour and a half, we cruised as the sun slowly dipped toward the horizon. We were served drinks of our choice—mine was a chilled white wine—and a platter of cheese, salami, and various dips, including hummus and spicy avocado. The sunset was, suffice to say, splendid.

I met an Australian couple. The man was a highly paid coal miner, and his striking wife worked at Commonwealth Bank. Later, I learned they were of Serbian origin and had known each other since their teenage years. It reminded me of my story with Talyn. How far I had come. I had always been a sucker for a romantic story, but this evening, I found myself happy in my own company. The old narratives of romantic love were just that—old stories. I wanted new stories and new forms of love.

Friday morning promised a full day of adventure with Cruise Whitsundays on their Whitehaven Chill and Grill tour. Departure was set for 8:30 a.m. On the journey out, I had tea and a chocolate biscuit and met a lovely young Aussie family with two small children. Though we were on the same boat, we were on different tours.

The large catamaran cruised through the Whitsunday Islands, and within an hour, we reached Whitehaven Beach, where we would spend the next six hours. We went on guided walks to Hill Inlet and Whitehaven Beach lookouts, then enjoyed a gourmet barbecue—a burger with a sesame bun, cucumber, beetroot ketchup, and a chicken wrap with a Coke. I sat at a table with two couples, one Japanese and one Uruguayan.

Just as I was finishing my meal, I felt something large and wet hit my hand—a seagull had excreted on me. I wondered what kind of luck the universe was bestowing upon me.

Later, I met a retired English couple from Leicester who were on a globe-trotting tour, with Australia as one of their stops. After chatting for a while, they put on their wetsuits and went for a swim. I preferred to feel the water directly on my skin, so I waded in up to my swimsuit, mindful of jellyfish and lemon sharks.

Again, I found it remarkable that I no longer felt the need to be with someone. For the first time, I was truly happy in my own skin. No people-pleasing, no competition—just me.

Saturday morning, after breakfast, I went back to my room and called Jack, my younger brother. It was 11:00 p.m. in London, and Jack was already fast asleep when I woke him up. Clearly, his new dog, Cleo, was exhausting him. I apologized and ended the call. I then called Chris, my youngest brother, who was in his car on the way to a meeting. He was pleased to hear from me, and we bantered for about 20 minutes.

Today, I'm taking it easy after yesterday's exhausting experience. I took the green bus to the marina and sat at a table outside the marina café, enjoying a peach iced tea while writing in my journal. As I observed the women passing by, I noticed that all of them were beautiful in their own way. Some fit the narrow standard of beauty that advertising has conditioned us to believe is perfection—an ideal that often feels unreal. I reflected on this concept of beauty, which, in many ways, is akin to idol worship. When we idealize an image, the actual person becomes irrelevant. We project onto them what we *want* them to be rather than seeing them for who they truly are. In doing so, we cheat ourselves—our authentic selves.

I'm tired of cheating myself. I'm tired of projecting qualities onto women that they do not possess. I'm tired of pleasing everyone at my own expense. I want to be authentic. I want genuine friendships and real relationships. While I'm grateful for all the people who have been part of my life over the past 69 years, I now must let them go. I can't do it overnight—it's a process—but it must be done.

I'm in the flow now, so I continue journaling.

In this next chapter of my life, I must let go of the people who no longer serve me, just as I no longer serve them. I am grateful for their past friendship, but I must release them with love and gratitude. I am learning to accept myself—physically, mentally, emotionally, and, above all, spiritually.

Accepting myself doesn't mean there's no room for growth. It simply means I will no longer allow negative, critical thoughts to take root in my mind. I can't control my thoughts as they arise, but I *can* control how I react to them. I can choose not to give them oxygen. I am becoming comfortable in my own skin.

Most people around me here are couples, many with children. I see the sacrifices both men and women make, the way they put others before themselves. I was once in that position. Of course, it's not just about responsibilities—there is also deep love and joy in spending time with one's children, especially on vacations. But now, my daughters are adults, living their own lives. My role as a father must evolve.

I've realized I am not the father I was programmed to be. If I have another 25 years ahead of me, I cannot simply drift into oblivion.

The year 2023 was the most challenging year for me and Talyn. It was a slow unraveling—our marriage, our lives—until we quietly divorced to preserve our friendship and our love for our daughters. Now, with my "Around the World in Eighty

Days" journey, I am creating the space and time to reinvent myself. Visiting new places, meeting new people, experiencing new possibilities.

Scary? Yes. Exciting? Yes. But you cannot have one without the other.

I don't know if I'm ready for a new relationship yet. That said, I sense that when the time comes, it will be different. I will need more solitude to balance my life. Solitude is essential for a rich spiritual existence. I need it as much as I need air and water.

I just came across a quote by Rumi:

> *"Do not worry that your life is turning upside down. How do you know the side you're used to is better than the one that is to come?"*

Just as I wrote this, I overheard an Australian mother—blonde, wearing a ponytail and a floral dress—chastising her adolescent son, who was taller than she was.

"I can't ignore the text I just received about your grandmother. She needs my help. Your needs and your enjoyment are not my priority right now."

Then, raising her voice, she added, "You need to understand that the world doesn't revolve around you. Do you understand me?"

My heart went out to her. I knew exactly how she felt. I'd been in that position with my daughters. That said, the feelings of the adolescent—just like those of my daughters—were just as valid. I had never been able to express my viewpoint as clearly as this woman had.

Talyn, my ex-wife, has been part of my life for 40 years. Four decades of shared experiences, not just as a couple, but as parents. Over those decades, our marriage evolved through many iterations—until there was no more elasticity, and the wrapper finally tore.

The rupture became unavoidable in 2015 when we couldn't agree on how to resolve our financial challenges. I ended up doing a 30-day silent retreat in North Wales, seeking a new path for myself. That retreat changed how I processed things.

We both began to grow—but in that growth, we also started to grow apart.

Neither of us was ready for a breakup.

Raised Catholic, I had been conditioned to believe that divorce was unthinkable. It was a family trauma—I had an uncle who divorced in the early 1960s, and the impact of that event echoed through the generations.

Although our divorce didn't take place until 2023, our marriage had been unraveling for eight years.

Everything has changed, and yet, nothing has changed. The marriage wrapper is gone, but a 40-year relationship cannot simply be erased. All control is gone. And surrender, I've found, is a relief.

All my life, I was attached to control—our home, our relationship, our shopping, our chores. Our marriage was a long-term investment I was unwilling to jettison. But I have come to see that the *marriage* had reached its expiration date, while the *relationship* remained. We are still parents to our two daughters. In life, we always have a choice. And no matter the choice, pain is unavoidable. We could have chosen to destroy our relationship entirely, harming both ourselves and our children. Or we could choose to repurpose our relationship, avoiding long-term hostility, bitterness, and resentment.

For me, the choice was obvious.

What else am I attached to? I'm attached to having someone familiar around me—the comfort of knowing I am not alone in the world. Yet, strangely, I sometimes felt lonelier when I was married than I do now. Like anyone, I am attached to habits and mindsets. But both have changed and continue to change. I am now open to possibilities, to uncertainties, to failures, and to the judgments of others. I am stronger than I first thought.

I woke up on Sunday morning, excited for an all-day snorkeling trip to Bates Reef in the Great Barrier Reef. As I lined up to board the catamaran, they couldn't find my name on the list. I had to walk to their office, where I was informed that the excursion had been canceled the day before due to high swells. They had tried to contact me, but they had no phone number or email for me.

I could have exploded, but instead, I chose to stay calm and Zen, convincing myself that the universe had a better plan for me. I opted for a half-day snorkel near Chalkie's Beach on Hazelwood Island, followed by a half-day visit to Whitehaven Beach on Whitsunday Island.

On the catamaran, a young instructor, Georgina Reilly, helped us prepare for our one-hour snorkel. It was fine, but nowhere near as magical as the one my daughter Elizabeth and I did on Exuma Island in the Bahamas when she was 15.

I also met Mikko, a sports coach; his wife, Alicia, a South African and a partner at a large consulting firm; and their autistic son, Indi, who had long blond curly hair. A lovely family. I had seen them earlier at breakfast at the Reef View Hotel—Alicia was feeding Indi yogurt by spoon while he was absorbed in his iPad, uncooperative. Strangely, at that very moment, I had been watching an Instagram meme of an osprey feeding her reluctant chick.

After our snorkel, we enjoyed a decent meal onboard the catamaran and then headed for Whitehaven Beach. Upon arrival, Mikko set off on a twelve-mile walk, while I opted for a shorter three-mile trek. Then, I had a cider and took a swim, still wearing my wetsuit.

Earlier in the morning, when we had traveled out of Hamilton and onto open waters, the swell was strong, and we bounced for 20 minutes before entering Solway Pass to reach Chalkie's Beach. By 2:30 p.m., when we boarded the catamaran for our return to Hamilton, the swell had intensified with the winds, forcing us to take the long way around—circling Whitsunday Island, passing Tumby Bay, crossing Hook Island to the north, and then making our way back down the other side of Whitsunday Island to reach Hamilton.

Once back, I headed straight to the hotel bookings desk to arrange a morning flight over the Great Barrier Reef on a fixed-wing plane, as Mikko had recommended. For A$380, I would have had an incredible aerial view. Sadly, no flights were available for the next morning. Only a helicopter was an option—at a staggering A$795 per person, requiring a minimum of two passengers, making it A$1,600. I politely declined. Perhaps the universe wanted me to return another time for that experience.

Today was my daughter Victoria's 35th birthday. I called her, and we chatted for a while.

On Monday morning, after breakfast, I went for a long walk, returned to the Reef View Hotel, paid my bill, and boarded the shuttle at 11:00 a.m. for my 12:45 p.m. flight to Melbourne, with a layover in Sydney.

At the airport, I was informed that my flight to Sydney was delayed by 30 minutes, which affected my connecting flight to Melbourne. After a long day of travel, I finally arrived at my hotel in Melbourne, Laneways by Ovolo, at 7:30 p.m.

Exhausted, I showered and was fast asleep by 8:30 p.m.

CHAPTER 6

Melbourne
16th – 20th April

I had arranged to have breakfast with Stephen Huppert, an Australian actuary. We met at the Little Gordon Café, opposite my hotel, housed in a former rectory. I had connected with Stephen online after reading his white paper, "Retirement Matters," for the Institute of Actuaries of Australia. His paper highlighted the limitations of financial planning and the significance of the non-financial aspects of retirement—an area few in the industry addressed. We discussed the possibilities of working together in both the short and long term, then parted ways.

I walked 20 minutes to Federation Square to a café called Time Out for a 10:00 a.m. meeting with Melinda, a guide for the Lanes and Arcade Tour. A devout Melburnian, Melinda pointed to the tall city building with a gold square on top, which commemorates Australia's gold rush—the very reason Melbourne was founded. It was named after the then-shortest-serving UK Prime Minister, Lord Melbourne (a title now claimed by Liz Truss). She confirmed that Melbourne and Sydney each have populations just over five million. She then gestured toward the magnificent Flinders Street Station, one of the most iconic railway stations in the world, with trains connecting Melbourne to its suburbs and exurbs. "Flinders Street Station is to Melbourne what the Opera House is to Sydney," she said. "It's our city's icon."

We explored a dozen lanes and alleys—just a fraction of the thousand-plus hidden throughout Melbourne. Many had been transformed into vibrant food courts and restaurants with outdoor seating, shaded by large umbrellas and warmed by heaters. We passed through Chinatown, established by a large Chinese community drawn to the gold rush. Coffeehouses here take their craft seriously; Starbucks has barely gained a foothold, unable to compete with the locals. In designated areas, graffiti is encouraged, elevating it to an art form. Some artists, like Vexta, have even gained recognition.

The Block Arcade, the most prestigious since its inception, was where wealthy Melburnian women once shopped and socialized over tea, ensuring they were seen "going around the block." The original Singer Sewing Machine Shop is now a tearoom, and the floor mosaics remain exquisite in both color and design.

Next, we visited the Royal Arcade, equally elegant with its covered glass roof and black-and-white floor tiles. A large clock, held aloft by Gog and Magog, was modeled after the figures at London's Guildhall. The former post office had been repurposed into an H&M, and the old stock exchange was now home to a branch of ANZ Bank, which had restored its original grandeur—ceiling decorations showcasing the coats of arms of London, Scotland, Ireland, and England, as well as polished mosaic floors and stained-glass windows. Another part of the building now housed an upscale French restaurant.

After the three-hour tour ended at 1:00 p.m., I went to Brunelli, an old Italian restaurant established in 1956 by a pâtissier who had come for the Melbourne Olympics and decided to stay. I enjoyed a delightful fettuccine al ragu with a glass of Valpolicella, then treated myself to a Ben & Jerry's hazelnut ice cream on a cone before heading back to the hotel for a rest.

As I walked through the city, I noticed billboards and shopfronts advertising the Melbourne International Comedy Festival, taking place across numerous venues. That evening, at 5:30 p.m., I set off for the Elephant and Wheelbarrow pub on Exhibition Road, just minutes from my hotel. At 6:15 p.m., three British comedians were set to perform in "Keep Calm: It's British Comedy." The show was excellent, though some of the coarser jokes managed to offend a few in the audience. The host, a brash woman, took particular pleasure in picking on me as a "Pom" and even called me a "c*nt" several times—a term Australians throw around as liberally as the British. Her problem, not mine, so I let it go.

After an enjoyable hour of comedy, I went for dinner at an Indian restaurant called Daughter-in-Law—an example of the wry Aussie humor even Indian restaurateurs adopt. I ordered tandoori chicken, but what arrived was a massive portion of grilled chicken with no trace of the vibrant orange hue typical of a proper tandoori dish in the UK. It looked like it had been cooked on a grill rather than in a tandoor oven. When I pointed this out to the chef, he apologized and offered to cancel my bill.

Wednesday morning did not start as planned. I was waiting at Her Majesty's Theatre at 9:45 a.m. for the Australian Wine Tour Company to pick me up. Half an hour later, a burgundy-colored minibus with the company's name emblazoned on its side finally appeared, and we set off for the Yarra Valley wineries. I was annoyed at the delay but decided not to give it oxygen and let it go.

After an hour and 15 minutes, we arrived at Yering Farm Wines, a small family-run vineyard producing wines for local consumption. We sampled their Sauvignon Blanc, Chardonnay, and signature Cabernet Sauvignon, The George, named after the owner's father. Lastly, we tried Traitor's Gate, a Shiraz named after vines originally planted by a former employee. The wines were unremarkable, but their cider—made from Pink Lady apples—was the most delicious cider I had ever tasted. It was called Farmyard Apple Cider.

Our next stop was the Balgownie Estate, a winery that also hosted a restaurant and spa. Our Polish wine presenter, Zenon, guided us through the autumn tasting selection, beginning with a sparkling wine, followed by a Sauvignon Blanc and a nouveau rosé. The final two tastings were Shiraz, one a deep, bold red and the other a sparkling Shiraz, nicknamed "the party drink" for its surprisingly high 14 percent alcohol content. We then moved to Restaurant 1309, where floor-to-ceiling windows framed stunning vineyard views. There, we enjoyed a set lunch paired with various wines.

At Rochford, our third winery, we sampled five wines: a Sauvignon Blanc, a Chardonnay, a Pinot Noir, a Syrah, and a rich, fortified Shiraz. They were all enjoyable, though none stood out as exceptional.

Our final visit was to Soumah, where a knowledgeable yet overly theatrical 23-year-old wine presenter took us through their selections. While his passion was evident, his showmanship distracted from the experience, and he failed to sell a single bottle to our group. His enthusiasm reminded me of my own youthful exuberance. We tasted their Chardonnay, Al Fiore, Rosario Pinot Noir, a heavy Syrah known as "The Butcher," and a Cabernet bearing the owner's family name. The highlight was the Bianchetto Frizzante, which had delicate notes of Turkish delight, rosewater, and strawberries—truly sublime. By the time I returned to my hotel, it was already dark. Overall, it had been a most enjoyable day.

Thursday morning, I was up at 6:00 a.m. for an early start at 7:30 a.m. The front desk had arranged a light bag breakfast, which had been placed outside my door the night before. After eating, I showered and was ready to go. A minivan was already parked outside at 7:20 a.m., with no other passengers yet. The driver and guide introduced himself as Gary—"The Great Gary" to his friends. We picked up an Indian couple from Toronto and, to my surprise, an American couple from Buffalo whom I had met on the Lanes and Arcades tour.

On our way to the Great Ocean Road, The Great Gary insisted we see kangaroos, so we stopped at a golf course where a few were lounging. However, our visit was cut short when a golf club attendant firmly chased us off the property.

Our first official stop was at a high vantage point overlooking the start of the Great Ocean Road, where we watched frothy waves lash the shore and saw students in wetsuits preparing to surf. We then visited the memorial dedicated to the servicemen who built the road after both world wars. A stop at Teddy's Lookout Point provided a spectacular view of the coastline stretching into the distance.

At 12:30 p.m., we had lunch at the Apollo Bay Hotel, named after a ship, that had been marooned there. I had fish and chips with a glass of local white wine. Back in the minibus, we spotted a koala perched on a tree, then watched another one leap from branch to branch.

Driving onward, we entered the Great Otway National Park—a dense rainforest—and as if on cue, the rain started.

Holding umbrellas over our heads, we walked among towering trees, some of which had massive hollows created by lightning strikes. When these trees eventually fell, they often took several others down with them. I came across a myrtle beech tree over 200 years old, its trunk formed from three trees that had grown together. We also saw a mountain ash and a towering eucalyptus regnans, known to reach heights of 100 meters.

Further along, we reached the Twelve Apostles, a collection of limestone stacks rising dramatically from the ocean. Originally called "The Sow and Its Piglets," they were later renamed by the Australian Tourism Board—perhaps borrowing inspiration from the ones in Cape Town, South Africa.

At the end of the Great Ocean Road, in Port Campbell, some 300 kilometers from Melbourne, The Great Gary took us to the gorge where the Loch Ard ship had wrecked in 1878. Of the 54 people on board, only two survived: Tom Pearce, the ship's apprentice, and Eva Carmichael, an 18-year-old Irish immigrant. Tom was swept into the gorge, clinging to an upturned lifeboat. Shortly after reaching the shore, he heard cries and saw Eva struggling in the water. He swam out to rescue her, and the two sheltered in a cave until morning. The next day, Tom found help, and both were saved. Tom went on to become a ship captain, and Eva went on to have a large family. A gripping story—though not the romantic ending many might have hoped for.

By the time I was dropped off at my hotel, it was early evening. The day had lasted 12 hours, covering over 600 kilometers.

Friday did not go as planned, but as you may have gathered, I am now more flexible and adaptable. I had intended to explore the coastal walk from Brighton Beach to Saint Kilda, but after yesterday's rain, the skies still looked ominous. The quickest way to Brighton Beach, with its colorful beach boxes, was by Uber. I typed in my destination; the cost was $35 each way. My heart wasn't in it. These days, I listen to my heart first.

Instead, I went across the road to Little Gordon for breakfast—chorizo and chili-infused scrambled eggs with my usual long black. Then, I decided to walk to Flinders Street. On the way, I stopped at the Scottish Church, where I saw a plaque dedicated to Dame Nellie Melba, the world-famous soprano from Melbourne. I passed by the Flinders statue on the lawn outside Saint Paul's Church, the city's premier Anglican church.

The night before, I had read about Captain Matthew Flinders, the great British navigator who circumnavigated Australia and Tasmania. His life was extraordinary. He married his childhood sweetheart but was separated from her for a decade after being wrongly imprisoned in Mauritius by its French governor, a supporter of Napoleon.

I continued to the National Gallery of Victoria, but as it wouldn't open for another hour, I decided to keep walking to my next destination: the Museum of Immigration. I spent an hour touring the history of immigration into Australia. In the 1850s, clipper ships from England to Australia took 70 to 80 days to make the journey. In the 1900s, steamships took 40 to 50 days to make the same crossing. In the 1950s, ocean liners took 30 days, whereas Qantas Empire Airways took about 60 hours. Between the 1970s and 1990s, Qantas Boeing 747 took 23 to 28 hours. Interestingly, in the 2000s, refugees taking buses, planes, and boats took between 6 and 24 months to enter Australia. What struck me as most interesting was that Australia only became a nation as late as 1901, when six of its colonies—New South Wales, Victoria, Queensland, South Australia, Western Australia, and Tasmania—united to form the Commonwealth of Australia, a process known as the Federation. One of the first acts of this Federation was the introduction of the Immigration Restriction Act—known as the White Australia Policy, which is self-explanatory. Between 1901 and 1945, Australia's mantra was "One nation, one people, one destiny," as most immigrants still came from Great Britain and Ireland. Immigration from continental Europe, Asia, and the Middle East was restricted to relatively small numbers, with quota numbers. After the devastation of the Second World War, Australia was unable to recruit from the homeland as Britain needed all its manpower, so they realized that they needed to "populate or perish." As late as 1966, Australia formally ended its White Australia Policy and opened the gates to immigration for skilled people who could contribute to Australia's growth.

I then spent another hour, captivated by the museum's focus on identity, a theme that resonated deeply with me and my work.

*   *   *

We often use labels as a form of personal shorthand. We make snap judgments about people and assume we know them, but do we really? Are labels helpful or misleading? As I journaled, I reflected on this.

What we are called:
Our names can be a blessing or a burden. When I went to boarding school in England at the age of 10, our family name was difficult to pronounce and even harder to spell. It was originally spelled DJERDJIAN because, back in 1896, my grandfather, who studied chemistry at Zurich Polytechnic in Switzerland, had to spell it phonetically for German speakers. In 1969, my father simplified it by dropping the D and officially changing it by deed poll to JERJIAN. At school, this

embarrassed me—it only drew more attention to my already well-established foreignness.

On one hand, I had been taught to be proud of my Armenian heritage. But as I integrated into school in England, that heritage became a handicap in my effort to fit in. "You have an exotic name. Where do you come from?" These questions made me cringe, reinforcing the feeling that, no matter what I did, I was never "English enough." My Armenian name was Kevork (Gevorg), but by the time I went to boarding school, I had dissociated from it. Today, I embrace it as part of my identity, using it as my online username.

Where we come from:
At school, I marveled at how my best friend, Robert Clifford-Holmes, could trace his ancestry all the way back to 1066 and William the Conqueror. I, on the other hand, could barely trace mine beyond my grandfather. It left me feeling inadequate. Decades later, I took matters into my own hands, researching my family history and eventually writing three books on it. That process brought me great satisfaction—not just for myself, but for my wider family and community. In doing so, I was able to exorcise my genealogical insecurity. Now, I feel complete.

Fast forward to today, and I no longer want to be like anyone else. I've also learned that what truly matters isn't where you come from but where you're going. Even more important is the journey itself—a sacred pilgrimage.

We all have different skin tones, different hair colors, different heights, noses, and eyes. Every day, we judge others, just as we judge ourselves. Back in 1968, at my English boarding school, I was one of only three foreigners—the other two were British boys who simply lived abroad. My skin was a darker shade of white than the pale complexions of my English classmates. I found it ironic that "Caucasian" was a term used for pale white people when my ancestors, the Armenians, were the original Caucasians, who lived in the shadow of the Caucasus Mountains.

My hair was dark brown and coarse, not blonde and soft. My nose was, I'm told, Roman, but not aquiline. My thick black glasses earned me the nickname "Roy Orbison," which I found offensive at the time. Years later, I would have been proud of the comparison, but back then, it stung. At five foot eight, I was considered too short to be an aristocrat like Robert, but just tall enough to make the rugby team. I was judged harshly, and in turn, I absorbed that judgment and projected it onto others. It did not serve me well.

What we say, and how we say it, speaks volumes about us—if we are aware and awake.

Language shapes how people think and feel. We take our own language for granted—until we find ourselves in a country where we don't understand a word. Our words connect us—to our identity, our family, our literature, our humor, even our dreams.

Language and accents also separate us, even within our own countries. When we hear people speaking in a foreign tongue, we instinctively wonder: *are they talking about me?* If we lose our language, we lose part of ourselves.

I was born to an Armenian family in Sudan, so my first languages were Armenian and Arabic. After the age of 10, English became my primary language, while the others atrophied. At prep school, I struggled with English at first. I hated reading because I couldn't fully understand it—my comprehension was weak. But I excelled in mathematics, because the language of numbers made sense to me. Eventually, though, English became my strongest language.

Even as my Armenian proficiency faded, I retained an emotional attachment to the language—especially to the Ter Voghormia (Lord, have mercy), a hymn I would hear at Armenian church services in Khartoum. Whenever I heard it, my spirit would rise, even as I welled up with emotion. As Leo Tolstoy once wrote, "Music is the shorthand of emotion."

At school, I read that the English poet Lord Byron had spent months on the island monastery of San Lazzaro in Venice, home to an Armenian Catholic monastic order, learning Armenian from the monks. After listening to their devotional singing, he wrote that Armenian was the language to speak to God. When I read that, I knew I wasn't imagining the deep connection I felt.

Another language I learned in my pre-teen years in Switzerland was French. I had an ear for it and loved it. Spending 35 summers in Nice, France, where my parents had an apartment facing the sea, only deepened my affection for the language. French, to me, was sexy, sophisticated—and a chick magnet to boot. Today, I rarely speak it, and I suspect that with it, I may have lost my chick magnetism.

Even my English accent influences how people perceive me. In Britain, an accent reveals one's background and social standing. Though I don't look Anglo-Saxon, I speak with what is known as received pronunciation—the educated accent of the British elite. When I lived in the US in the 1980s, Americans often complimented me on my accent, which in some ways betrays the reality of my upbringing.

What we wear:
Clothing does more than just cover us—it reveals what we like, what we can afford, what we believe in, and what we aspire to.

Brand names, colors, textures, styles, and cosmetics all project an image.

Even in adolescence, I was known for sartorial elegance, which my less stylish classmates teased me about. For decades, I bought only branded clothing. My watches, glasses, cuff links, scents, jackets, and shoes were all high-end, and I rarely gave anything away.

But about five years ago, I changed. I sold most of my watches and donated much of my wardrobe to British Red Cross and Oxfam. Now, I own:

- Three suits
- Four quality shirts
- Two pairs of leather shoes
- A black cashmere coat

My wardrobe is now a limited, versatile uniform. I also wear an Apple Watch by day and a Cartier watch on special evenings. My glasses are all Moscot, so I don't have to buy new lenses—an expensive necessity for someone as short-sighted as I am.

With my pared-down wardrobe, I can adapt my look while staying within my personal style. My glasses hint at my studious nature. But my tattoos—two large ones on my upper arms and smaller script on my lower arms—confuse people.

Tattoos, after all, break taboos. Some of my old friends are shocked, but in my new life, I am an activist and a reformer. I must change what I project.

Yet, I remain authentic. I still love good quality clothing and accessories—just in a more mindful, minimalist way.

What we eat:
The food we eat does more than nourish us—it reflects our tastes, beliefs, and cultural backgrounds. But are we really what we eat? In the past, dietary habits were used to distinguish people. No bacon or pork? They must be Jews or Muslims. Fish on Fridays? They must be Catholics.

Generally, I prefer eating healthy foods. I consume plenty of fruits, vegetables, fish, and chicken, with occasional servings of meat. I also love most cheeses, but due to my high cholesterol, I now stick mostly to sheep and goat cheese. While I do enjoy Chinese and Indian food, I often find myself gravitating toward sushi or Italian pasta. Ultimately, I eat to live, not live to eat.

My working life:
What does work mean to me? Throughout my career, I've been employed only a few times, and never for long. Even though I wanted to be part of something bigger—like my friends who held steady jobs—I've never been able to focus on work that is repetitive or uninspiring. My mind simply isn't wired that way. It's constantly churning, creating, and exploring, making it difficult to engage with anything monotonous.

I thrive on researching, writing, editing, teaching, and speaking—so that's the path I'm pursuing now. Over the years, I've worked in marketing, sales, financial services, real estate, and commercial litigation funding, but always in a self-employed capacity, with varying degrees of success.

For me, work is now a vocation. I help retirees unretire and embark on new beginnings. At the same time, I'm committed to lifelong learning, which is why I've undertaken this journey. Who knows what opportunities may come from it?

* * *

After leaving the Museum of Immigration, I decided to get a haircut. Using Google Maps, I found Oxbridge Barbershop on Little Collins Street. The young British woman from Cambridge who cut my hair had started the shop 12 years ago and was thriving in Melbourne. She gave me a buzz cut, as requested, to last me through the next five weeks in New Zealand and Japan.

Once I was finished, I craved a cappuccino and a croissant, so I grabbed both before heading to the City Circle tram, a free service that loops around the central business district. The tram, an old wooden one painted in green and yellow, offered a charming ride. After 90 minutes, hunger set in, so I looked up the best Indian restaurants nearby and landed on Chili India. I enjoyed a bowl of white rice, butter chicken, Rogan Josh lamb, cucumber yogurt, and a roti.

After lunch, I walked to the State Library of Victoria, a magnificent structure both inside and out. The ground floor was the centerpiece of the library, visible from all six floors above. In the center stood a high desk where the librarians were stationed, and extending outward were eight long wooden desks, forming a starburst shape. One of the upper floors featured an exhibition on books and writing through the ages, including displays on the Pharaohs, the Rosetta Stone, and the three Abrahamic religions.

Though I was tired, I had one last stop to make—the panoramic view of Melbourne from the Eureka Tower. Melinda, my guide from earlier in the week, had pointed it out as the building with the gold square on top. I walked over, bought my ticket, and took a silent turbo-charged elevator to the 88th floor in under two minutes. The view was not just spectacular—it was magical.

On Saturday morning, I prepared to head to Melbourne International Airport for my 1:30 p.m. Qantas flight to Auckland, New Zealand.
30 days completed.
50 days remaining.

PART 3

NEW ZEALAND

"New Zealand is a small country but a large village."

Peter Jackson
Director, Writer, Producer
Lord of The Rings Trilogy

New Zealand

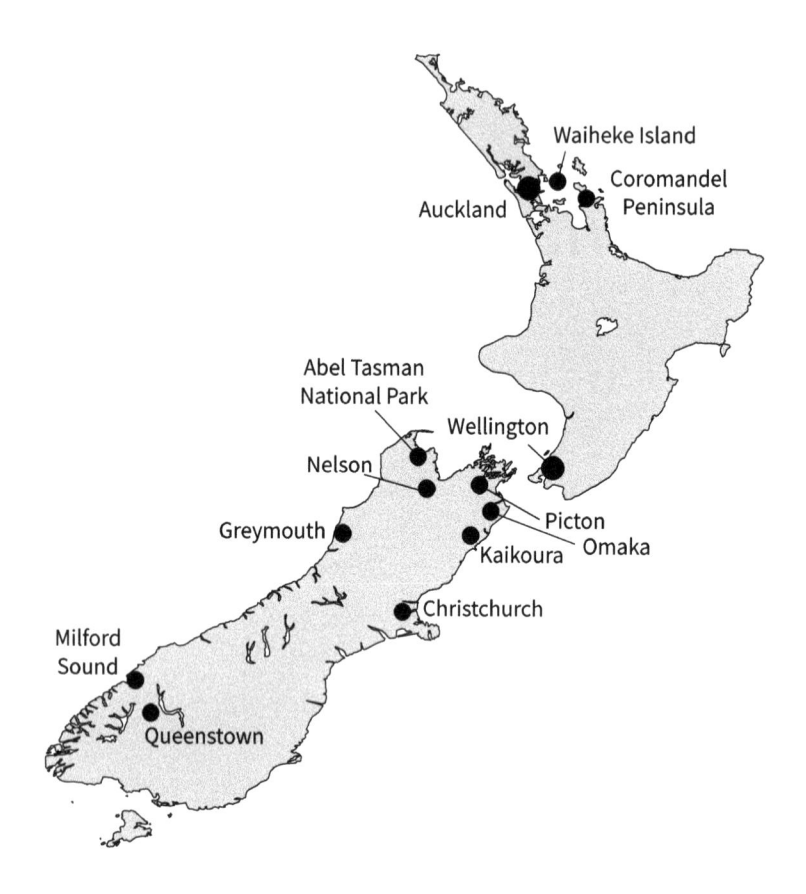

CHAPTER 7

NORTH ISLAND

Auckland
20th – 22nd April

On Saturday at 1:20 p.m., my Qantas flight departed Melbourne for Auckland, a journey of about three hours—the same time it takes to fly from New York to Miami. Factoring in the two-hour time difference, I arrived at the Britomart Hotel after 7:30 p.m. local time. Exhausted, I crashed before 10:00 p.m.

On Sunday, at the crack of dawn, I drew the curtains and saw a grey, rainy sky. Despite the dreary weather, the panorama of Auckland (population: 1.65 million)—with its harbors, Sky Tower, and general city layout—left a good impression. I was also struck by my hotel room, where the lighting, heating, and curtains were all electronically controlled, ergonomic, and economic.

After showering and dressing, I went downstairs for breakfast: scrambled eggs on sourdough with a long black, as an Americano is also known here. My half-day Waikiki Island Explorer tour was canceled due to the downpour. Unlike Melbourne's unpredictable four-seasons-in-a-day weather,

Auckland's skies looked set for a full-day rain, more like London. Without getting upset, I changed my plans. Museums it would be.

I walked to the Maritime Museum, which the concierge had recommended, but when I reached the doors, I saw that it didn't open until 10:00 a.m. A glance at my watch told me it was only 8:10 a.m. Disappointed, I wandered through the Central Business District, and my spirit sank at the soullessness of the place. Even Queen Street, lined with global fashion brands, felt lifeless. The number of homeless people sleeping in cardboard boxes was striking, and even the McDonald's franchise looked bleak. Was it the weather, the landscape, or me—or a combination of all three? I walked back to my hotel and retreated to my room.

After an hour of scrolling through social media, I ordered an Uber to the Auckland War Memorial Museum. Ten minutes later, the car approached the majestic grey-stone building, its front pillars reminding me of the Parthenon.

On the ground floor, there were exhibitions on Auckland's history and Māori civilization. I was drawn to a 30-minute Māori dance and song performance, which was deeply impressive. A Māori woman explained that their culture had no tradition of applause because they had no need for validation. Instead, if a performance resonated, we could express our appreciation by shaking our hands and wrists—a gesture she demonstrated. The performers showcased the poi dance and the haka—not the version made famous by the All Blacks rugby team, but the authentic haka.

This Māori rejection of validation left an impression on me, especially in contrast to our own culture, where approval is so deeply ingrained. It reminded me of conversations with my daughter Elizabeth, who has often told me she doesn't need validation from anyone to pursue what she wants. On this day, I fully agreed with her. I called to share what I had learned from Māori culture, and I like to think she was pleased to hear that I was evolving.

On the second floor, I explored halls dedicated to the origins of Māori culture, ancient civilizations, and volcanoes, or Mataaho. I also entered a specially designed earthquake simulation room. The experience began with a black-and-white television news broadcast reporting ominous warnings. Then came a loud explosion, followed by the roar of giant tsunami waves crashing over the house—our simulation room. It was hard not to feel a primal fear, even knowing it was a simulation.

I stepped out and recovered from the experience with a cup of Earl Grey and an Anzac biscuit.

The third floor housed war memorials and galleries commemorating the Boer War, World War I, World War II, and the Korean War, along with a library and auditorium. What amazed me was the sheer number of Kiwis (and Australians) who served in these wars for the British Empire. Relative to their populations, they sacrificed a higher percentage of their young men than Britain itself. As I traveled Down Under, I saw firsthand the deep emotional connection these nations still hold toward Britain.

After spending four hours in the museum, I left just after 2:00 p.m. and returned to my hotel to rest.

That evening, I had dinner with Mike Silverman, an old Kiwi friend from London whom I had known for a decade when we were both members of a Toastmasters Club, a global public-speaking organization. Our club, London Corinthians, was the second to be established in the city. Fast forward 30 years, and London now has 60 Toastmasters clubs.

Mike arrived at my hotel lobby at 7:00 p.m., and we walked to an Asian fusion restaurant called White + Wong's. We shared drunken noodles as a starter, followed by lamb massaman curry. It was a delightful evening of reminiscing and good food.

CHAPTER 8

Coromandel Peninsula
22ⁿᵈ – 24ᵗʰ April

Up at 7:30 a.m. on Monday morning, I showered, finished packing, and went downstairs for my usual scrambled eggs on sourdough bread and a long black. I phoned my daughter Elizabeth and spoke to her for five minutes, which lifted my spirits. Once I had paid the hotel bill for my extras, I ordered an Uber and headed to the Avis/Budget car rental office at Auckland Airport. I was given a grey Peugeot P3008—not an inspiring choice, but a practical one. I struggled to familiarize myself with the car's instruments, particularly the screen monitor, which I needed to connect to my phone's GPS via Google Maps. After some trial and error, I got it working and set off merrily on my journey to Coromandel.

    I had been driving for at least 90 minutes when I checked Google Maps and realized I had missed the turn that would take me to the Coromandel Peninsula (population: 33,700). I had lost about an hour, heading farther south than necessary. Frustrated, I reset my GPS and got back on track. On my way, however, it directed me onto what appeared to be a shortcut leading back to the highway toward Coromandel. This detour, called Island Block Road, took me through 11 miles of the most stunning countryside I had laid eyes on—rolling hills, lush farmland, cows, sheep, red barns, streams, and quaint little bridges. In the past, I would have been furious with myself for making such a basic mistake and wasting time. Not so now. It reminded me that when things go wrong, there is often a silver lining. If you lose your temper, if you let frustration take over, you risk missing the unexpected beauty right in front of you.

As I headed toward the town of Hahei, I found myself on the magnificent Hot Water Beach Road, which stretched for miles, meandering through mountains dense with forests and offering breathtaking views of the sea and river. My jaw dropped at several points, but with cars behind me and no safe place to pull over, I couldn't stop to take photos.

After just under four hours, I entered the town of Hahei and soon turned into the driveway leading to my hotel, The Church Hahei. The hotel was a reconstructed 1916 Methodist church, set within 1.5 acres of native bush and gardens. I parked near the reception, but no one was there—only a note with my name on it and a set of keys for Cottage Number 5, which would be my home for the next two days. The number five stood out to me, as in numerology, it represents change. Cottage Number 5 at The Church was beautiful yet spartan, with stained-glass windows that gave the room a monastic feel, much like my days at Douai Abbey in Berkshire, UK, where I used to go to write and edit my manuscripts. Dinner that evening was at the Church Bistro, operated by two Brazilian couples now living in New Zealand. The menu was nouvelle cuisine—exceptionally delightful.

On Tuesday morning, I woke up feeling cold, so I decided to skip my shower. I dressed quickly, and thankfully, the owners had provided a breakfast tray the night before. It contained muesli, yogurt, a local fruit—small like a guava but tasting more like a starfruit—two slices of toast with butter and honey, and a cup of tea. I savored every bite.

I then walked to the village center and continued past it toward the beach at Hahei. Near the shore, I noticed a woman in a wetsuit unloading gear from her car. Two other women soon joined her, and together, they made their way toward the sea for a morning swim. I marveled at the athleticism of these Kiwis. I reached a spot called The Point, the starting point of the Cathedral Cove Walk. I had been warned that the path to Cathedral Cove was no longer safe due to a recent storm that had caused landslides and rockfalls. I managed to hike to Cathedral Cove from the top via Grange Road, but when I reached the stairs leading down, they did not inspire confidence. Instead of risking the descent, I made my way back to the Hahei village coffee shop for a drink and a sweet treat. Afterward, I returned to my cottage to change into swimwear and flip-flops, ready for my 10-kilometer drive to Hot Water Beach.

At a shop called "Hotties," which made me chuckle, I rented a spade and a towel from a Kiwi woman with silver hair for NZ$20, leaving my car keys as a deposit. I walked several hundred yards to Hot Water Beach, where around 50 people—singles, couples, and families—had already dug holes in the sand and were lying in the warm water. I tried digging a few holes myself, but either freezing cold water seeped in, or the water was scalding hot.

I then approached a dugout where steam was rising above the surface. Before I could test it, a couple closer to my age invited me to join their large pool, which was pleasantly warm. I gladly accepted. The man was South African, and the woman was a Kiwi. We introduced ourselves and chatted about our respective countries and my travels. The beach, with its scattered dugouts, looked like a battlefield, but I was told that by the evening, the tide would wash everything away, restoring it to pristine condition for the next day's visitors.

After about 30 minutes, I was thoroughly cooked—quite literally—and ready to leave. I rose, dried myself with my towel, said my goodbyes, and returned my towel and spade to the Kiwi woman at Hotties. She pointed to her husband and said, "Mark, can you please help this gentleman?" Mark ran the bar and restaurant next door, which was officially closed. I asked if there was anywhere nearby to get food. He mentioned that although his bar wasn't open, he was making fish and chips for five workers and asked if I would be interested in the same. I accepted and enjoyed my meal, sitting by the beach and listening to the waves lapping the shore.

After 2:00 p.m., I returned to my cottage to shower, rest a bit, and then journal.

At 6:30 p.m., I went for dinner at the Church Bistro. I had a truffle risotto with bacon, followed by beef bourguignon with pasta, washed down with a local pinot noir. For dessert, I had a small apple custard pie with vanilla ice cream—mouth-wateringly delicious. On Wednesday, I woke up at 7:00 a.m. Having already paid my bill the night before, I was ready to leave early. Rather than having breakfast locally, I decided to head straight to Coromandel town and eat there. I packed my last-minute belongings, put my luggage in the trunk of my Peugeot, and said goodbye to Hahei.

I plugged my destination into Google Maps and was informed that my journey would take an hour and 15 minutes, meaning I would arrive at 9:30 a.m. As I drove, I noticed that the bonnet was completely wet, as though it had rained the night before, though I knew it hadn't. I was puzzled until I saw thick fog blanketing the mountains and valleys ahead. Eventually, I reached the fog and drove through it, but for a while, I worried that it might persist for miles. Thankfully, after about half an hour, it dissipated.

The drive was stunning. The landscape of the peninsula filled me with joy, and I felt an irresistible urge to stop and take photos and videos. However, the roads were narrow and steep, and at times, cars behind me forced me to keep moving. I managed to find three designated spots where I could pull over, and I was grateful for the opportunity to capture the breathtaking views.

At exactly 9:30 a.m., I arrived in Coromandel and parked in a designated spot. Searching for a meter, I asked a passerby and was delighted to learn that parking in this town was free. What a pleasure to be in a place where you don't have to pay for parking.

I entered a café called Umu and ordered scrambled eggs with bacon and toast, along with a long black. "A king's breakfast," I told the Māori girl who served me. After finishing my meal, I left Coromandel town at 10:00 a.m. and drove toward Waiomu, about 45 minutes south along the Pacific Coast Highway.

Upon arriving, I stopped at the Waiomu Beach Café, which Annie, the co-owner of The Church hotel in Hahei, had recommended. I ordered their carrot cake and enjoyed it, but their coffee was disappointing. After half an hour, I left to drive directly to Auckland Airport, an hour and 40 minutes away.

Today, the 24th of April, holds special significance for me for three reasons. First, it marks my parents' 70th wedding anniversary. Second, it is Anzac Day in New Zealand, a time to commemorate the sacrifice of 60,000 of its sons in World War I. Third, and closely connected to these two events, it is the 109th anniversary of the Armenian Genocide, which resulted in the killing of 1.5 million Armenians and the loss of their three-millennia-old homeland. Three weeks before April 24, 1915, Allied troops and ships were stationed outside the Bosporus Strait in Istanbul. Whether by fate or coincidence, my parents' marriage on April 24 seemed to create an ancestral call for me to engage in advocacy, striving to bring attention to this painful chapter in history and work toward a peaceful resolution.

After filling the car with a full tank of gas, I returned it to the Avis/Budget rental office at Auckland Airport just before 2:00 p.m. My flight to Wellington, the country's capital (population: 216,200), was not until 5:00 p.m., so I had plenty of time for lunch. I hadn't eaten at McDonald's in decades, but for some inexplicable reason, I felt a strong craving for a Big Mac with fries and a Coke. I decided to go with the impulse.

Later, when the check-in counters opened, I dropped off my luggage, received my boarding pass, and went through security to the boarding lounge. There, I sat down to journal, knowing I would be too exhausted to write by the time I checked into the Bolton Hotel in Wellington.

CHAPTER 9

SOUTH ISLAND

Nelson
25th – 27th April

Thursday morning, I woke up at 6:00 a.m. because a driver was set to pick me up an hour later to take me from the Bolton Hotel to the ferry terminal for the crossing to the South Island. I went down to the lobby, paid my bill, and was ready on time for the pickup. At the Wellington ferry terminal, I collected my pre-paid tickets, and an hour later, we began boarding the Interislander ferry, Kaitaki. I was ushered into a special lounge with large armchairs and a breakfast buffet.

I sat down and was soon joined by a Kiwi couple who introduced themselves as Jenni and Graham McDougall. Over breakfast, we shared our stories. Graham was first-generation English from Wellington, and Jenni, with silver hair down to her shoulders and a pair of blue plastic spectacles, was a sixth-generation Kiwi from Christchurch. Married for 47 years with four adult children, they were now retired and living near Queenstown. He was 70, a former structural engineer with his own business and a motor enthusiast, proud owner of both a Jaguar and an Aston Martin. When they learned that I would be in Queenstown and heading for Milford Sound, they invited me to lunch the following Friday.

Upon disembarking in Picton, I headed to the Avis/Budget car rental office, where I was given a navy-blue Mitsubishi Outlander. I set off immediately for my two-hour drive to Nelson (population: 52,900), the gateway to Abel Tasman National Park. I parked in the driveway of Cambria House, my lodgings for the next two nights. The landlady, Karel Wallace, welcomed me warmly and ensured that my planned activities were confirmed. My sailing trip had been canceled as the season was over, but I was offered a boat trip followed by a three-hour hike in Abel Tasman National Park. I accepted the change and was pleased with how things had worked out.

On Friday morning at 7:00 a.m., Karel served me a sumptuous English breakfast. In conversation, I discovered that she was a sixth-generation Nelsonian and that both she and her husband, who was away, had strong emotional ties to Scotland and England. From my own Armenian roots, I understood how distance from one's homeland creates a deep emotional connection that may not make sense to the rational mind.

By 7:30 a.m., I was out the door, driving my Outlander toward Kaiteriteri, an hour away from Nelson. My route took me through Richmond, Mapua, Tasman, Lower Moutere, Motueka, and Riwaka before navigating endless winding roads up and down until I finally reached Kaiteriteri. I parked my car and went to the office of Wilsons, one of the oldest operators in Abel Tasman National Park. I collected my tickets, bought a Reuben sandwich, a banana, and a berry shake for lunch, and forgot to get coffee before boarding the Vista catamaran.

I took a seat at the front of the catamaran. There was an empty spot between me and a sullen-looking young man, so I scrolled on my phone to pass the time. Soon, a petite and friendly young woman came and sat between us, causing the sullen man to suddenly perk up. She introduced herself as Soarse, a student from London, and he introduced himself as Martin, a student from Germany. I went downstairs to grab an Earl Grey tea and returned to my seat. We started chatting, but the skipper kept pointing out places of interest, so our attention shifted to snapping photos of dolphins and seals.

At 10:50, after several stops during the 90-minute ride, the catamaran reached the starting point of my walk: Tonga Quarry. I was dropped off on the beach alone and began hike number three, a pathway that wound up and down through a forest. The terrain alternated between smooth, rocky, and even sandy stretches. I paused occasionally to take in the surroundings, noticing the beauty of the vegetation—trees, palm trees, and bushes. The roar of the ocean below was constant, and glimpses of the blue and green waters peeked through the trees and shrubs. Later, I heard the sound of running water, and while crossing a steel bridge over a small stream, I saw a stunning waterfall.

Along the path, I encountered two cheerful hikers, Jenny and Alan from Tucson, Arizona, coming from the opposite direction. We stopped to chat for a few minutes. I also passed a few others—some friendly and smiling, others introspective and seemingly oblivious to my presence.

Midway through my hike, I found an impressive hut, open to the public. I stepped inside and had my lunch there. Later, I sat alone on a beach, facing the ocean and saying, "Lord, speak. Your servant is listening." I often do this. Sometimes, I hear something drop into my mind; other times, I hear nothing. Today, there was silence, but it felt good just being there.

I slowly made my way to Medlands Beach, my pickup point for the return trip at 3:10 p.m. The hike covered just over four kilometers, and I took my time, completing it at a leisurely pace in two and a half hours.

I arrived at Medlands Beach an hour early and perched on a rock to watch the waves. A young Dutch student named Laike arrived, and we struck up a conversation that lasted until we reached Kaiteriteri. I offered her a lift back, but she declined, so we said our goodbyes. Just then, I met Martin, Soarse, and a group of their friends. They invited me for drinks, and I joined them. I ordered a glass of pinot gris and a pepperoni pizza and chatted with a lovely student named Kyra Clement. After an hour, I had to leave—I needed to get back to Nelson before nightfall, as I prefer not to drive in the dark due to my poor eyesight.

On Saturday morning, I was up at 6:00 a.m., had breakfast at 7:00 a.m., and, knowing it was my last day, ensured I was packed and out of Cambria House by 7:30 a.m. I said goodbye to Karel and set off on a three-hour drive: from Nelson to Havelock via Route 6, then along the scenic Queen Charlotte Drive to Picton, where the ferry had dropped me off two days earlier. From Picton, I continued on Route 1 to Blenheim before turning southwest to the Omaka Aviation Heritage Centre, which Karel had highly recommended.

Sir Peter Jackson, the director, writer, and producer of *The Lord of the Rings* trilogy, was directly involved in the Omaka Aviation project, and I spent two fascinating hours looking at World War I and World War II airplanes and pilots. This was particularly interesting to me because of three World War I ace pilots—René Fonck, Charles Nungesser, and François Coli—who failed in their attempted transatlantic flights. Their loss to Charles Lindbergh, who successfully made the first nonstop transatlantic flight from New York to Paris on May 21, 1927, had always fascinated me.

A few years ago, I read Lindbergh's book, *The Spirit of St. Louis*, which was also the name of his airplane, and I connected deeply with the story for three reasons. First, the three World War I ace pilots were funded generously by New York's top bankers for their Atlantic crossing attempts, while Lindbergh was denied such support. Despite their resources, they failed because they lacked the resilience and ingenuity required for such a journey. Second, Lindbergh barely scraped together the funds from local bankers in St. Louis and went on to custom-build his plane in San Diego—a machine he described as "a large gas tank with wings." Third, my book, *Spirit of Gratitude*, is a homage to Charles Lindbergh. His Atlantic crossing was not just a physical feat but a mental and emotional one. It wasn't merely a crossing; it was a transition from who he was to who he was meant to become.

After leaving Omaka, I drove to a local Marlborough winery, Wither Hills, but they were fully booked for the weekend. However, the sommelier recommended The Vines Village for good food and wine. I followed his advice and enjoyed a delicious seafood platter, paired with a glass of Whitehaven rosé, finishing with a double espresso to ensure I stayed alert for the drive.

CHAPTER 10

Kaikoura
27th – 29th April

After lunch, I drove for just under two hours, nonstop on Route 1, from Blenheim through arid terrain that resembled a lunar landscape, before reaching the town of Kaikoura (population: 4,215) on the northeast coast of the South Island. I arrived at The Factory (formerly the Hapuku Co-operative Dairy Co.). Yes, that was the name of my hotel—a former dairy factory now converted into an industrial-chic hotel. A petite blonde Kiwi walked over from next door and introduced herself as "Skip" Gregory. She showed me to my room, which was enormous—more like a one-floor, luxurious house, with modern amenities and exceptional comfort. After confirming my dolphin expedition for the next day, I went to the nearby private beach for a stunning sunset just after 5:30 p.m., as Skip had recommended. The sky was painted in pink and blue brushstrokes, and the sand was dark grey, possibly volcanic ash. I walked along the shore, feeling so far away from everything I knew.

Back in my room, I felt too tired to go out for dinner. Fortunately, Skip had prepared a platter of salami slices, a small round of brie cheese, a cluster of red grapes, a selection of cheese biscuits, and a bottle of sparkling wine. I was grateful for a wonderful day.

On Sunday, I woke up at 6:00 a.m. after a good night's sleep. An hour later, Skip knocked on my door with a tray laden with a full English breakfast she had personally cooked. By 7:45, I was in my Outlander, driving 10 minutes to Dolphin Encounter at 96 Esplanade in Kaikoura. As I entered the building, I immediately noticed the efficiency and warmth of Kiwi hospitality. Operating for over 30 years, this company not only provided dolphin experiences for tourists but also ran a coffee shop and a high-end gift shop. Three young women managed the counter, processing all 25 customers quickly and cheerfully. The equipment—wetsuits, snorkels, flippers, and GoPro underwater cameras—was of high quality and well-maintained. Impressively, they even provided me with a snorkel with minus-seven lens correction for my short-sightedness, which promised to make this an even more enjoyable experience.

We were ushered into a small auditorium for an instructional video explaining how to put on our wetsuits, secure the headwrap, and fit our snorkels and flippers. We were also told that we should not touch the wild dolphins but instead mimic their swimming and make noises to attract them. The staff emphasized that swimming with dolphins was a privilege, not a right, setting a respectful tone and managing our expectations beautifully.

Before boarding the bus, we were already clad in our wetsuits. Once everyone had boarded the two buses, we set off to the other side of the peninsula, to South Bay, where two catamarans awaited us.

Out at sea, a pod of dolphins was spotted within 20 minutes. Our dolphin expert and leader, Faye, instructed us to sit on the two stairs at the back of the catamaran. She explained that when the captain stopped the engines and propellers, he would sound the horn, signaling us to descend gently into the water. With my right hand holding my GoPro camera, already recording, I slowly lowered myself into the refreshingly cool water. I kept my legs straight, moving them up and down alternately to keep my flippers flipping, while using my left hand to pivot left or right. I started making cooing noises to attract the dolphins. Within two minutes, a pair arrived and circled around me a few times. I tried to keep up with them, but they were far too fast. Then, to my shock and amusement, the pair engaged in a brief mating display right in front of me—a moment I caught on video. I had only been in the water five minutes, but I had already captured some amazing shots on camera.

Back on board, I told Faye about the dolphins' amorous encounter. She laughed and said they must have felt very comfortable around me. "Of course they did," I replied, "but I'm not quite ready for interspecies sex romps just yet." This led Faye to share some fascinating insights into the sex lives of dolphins, who, as it turns out, are highly promiscuous. Female dolphins mate with multiple males—sometimes up to five—so paternity would be difficult to determine if they had a legal system and lawyers. Pregnancies last up to 11 months, after which female dolphins form a communal "crèche" with other mothers, as they typically have only one calf at a time. The calf stays with its mother for up to two years, learning to hunt before being encouraged to become independent. At this point, females return once again to the dating scene.

Among our group were several young Korean students, including one girl who did not swim but still managed to capture some stunning videos of dolphins swimming, jumping, and somersaulting. She kindly shared a few of them with me.

By noon, we were back at Dolphin Encounter's offices. One of the staff members helped me download my video footage to my phone, and I left glowing feedback for the company and for Faye in particular.

By then, I was starving. I followed Faye's recommendation and headed to a roadside shack by the sea called the Kikori Seafood Barbecue Shack. I had the fish of the day—grouper—served with rice, salad, and garlic bread, followed by a vanilla and coffee-flavored ice cream cone. It was the perfect end to an unforgettable morning.

CHAPTER 11

Christchurch
29th April – 1st May

On Monday, I was up at 7:00 a.m., already washed, dressed, and packed, waiting for Skip to bring my breakfast at 8:00 a.m. This day carried a memory: it was 41 years ago this evening that Talyn, my ex-wife, and I had our engagement dinner at the Ritz Hotel in Piccadilly, London. I reflected on that day consciously, free from the guilt and shame that once defined my recollections. I still loved her. Decades of habits are hard to shake, but not impossible.

I hear the roar of the ocean and feel at home. New Zealand is breathtaking and welcoming, but it is far from everything I know. I recall feeling the same way about Hawaii during my first visit in 1988. Now, with thoughts of mortality ever present, I cherish my independence and solitude, preferring to be connected to many communities rather than anchored to just one.

Another part of me longs for companionship, for someone I'm drawn to—someone who makes me feel wanted and needed. But not yet. Perhaps dolphins, intelligent creatures that love to play, hold the answer.

I said my goodbyes and thanked Skip a few minutes before 9:00 a.m. before setting off for Christchurch, a 125-mile drive that would take about three hours with stops.

The day was beautiful, and driving through New Zealand felt like a true vacation. With my window open for fresh air, I drove for 90 minutes before stopping at Number Eight Café in Cheviot. I had a cappuccino and a moist carrot cake muffin. After 15 minutes, I was back on the road. Just before leaving, I heard a ping and checked my emails. A message from Pacific Destinations informed me of some complications regarding my TranzAlpine journey the next day. I managed to sort it out on the spot before continuing.

I arrived in Christchurch (population: 396,200) at 12:45 p.m. and drove to my hotel, Eliza's Manor, where the manager, Russ, checked me into my room, The Canterbury. The name took me back to my school days studying Chaucer's *Canterbury Tales*.

Shortly after settling in, I received a text from my friend Mike Silverman from Auckland. He and his wife, Izzy, had unexpectedly flown to Christchurch to look after their grandchildren for a few weeks. As it turned out, I had just arrived, so we met for sandwiches and drinks before they showed me around the city center by car. From what I could see, Christchurch—devastated by a major earthquake in 2011—had made an astonishing recovery. It was a city that had risen from the rubble.

That evening, I had an early dinner with Anna Harper of talljourney.com, whom a mutual friend had connected me by an email introduction. We met at Kum Pun Thai on 73 Victoria Street at 5:30 p.m. and, coincidentally, both ordered the same dish—a green curry with seafood—paired with a Good Shepherd pinot noir. After a wonderful two-and-a-half-hour conversation, I returned to Eliza's Manor.

On Tuesday, I woke at 6:30 a.m., washed, dressed, and ate the breakfast box provided the night before—a kiwi fruit, a croissant, and a bowl of yogurt with muesli. At 8:00 p.m. London time, I called my mother's carer, Michelle, to check in, but my mother was already asleep.

My Uber arrived promptly at 7:20 a.m. and took me to Christchurch Railway Station. I left my blue baseball cap in the Uber but hoped to recover it when the driver picked me up upon my return. At the station, I secured my return tickets, and soon after, the train doors of our KiwiRail TranzAlpine train opened. We departed at 8:15 a.m.

The first hour was typical of train travel out of a city—dreary urban landscapes, followed by quiet suburban sprawl. After passing Rolleston, Darfield, Sheffield, and Springfield, the scenery became more dramatic. Beyond Cass, we encountered Mount White and the mighty Waimakariri River, fast-flowing and ice blue. For the next 10 kilometers, the train followed the river, and I stood on the observation deck at the front of the train, snapping photos and taking videos nonstop.

At 10:40 a.m., we reached Arthur's Pass station, the halfway point of our journey and the entrance to a five-mile tunnel through the mountains. We disembarked for five minutes to stretch our legs. When the horn blared, we reboarded, and the train entered the Otira Tunnel—the second-longest in the world at 8.5 kilometers (5.3 miles). Constructed between 1908 and 1923 with the help of returning servicemen, it runs beneath the Southern Alps from Arthur's Pass to Otira.

Just after noon, we passed Lake Brunner on our left, a serene expanse set against mountains veiled in clouds. It reminded me of how I imagined Lake Lucerne, in Switzerland, in the 1960s.

By 1:00 p.m., we arrived in Greymouth, our destination on the opposite coast from Christchurch. With an hour for lunch before the return journey, I struck up a conversation with Ollie Cochran, a photographer from Dublin who also happened to be 69. We ate at Robert Harris Café, where he insisted on buying my lunch—a chicken, apricot, and cream cheese panini with a hot drink.

Ollie shared that he was a widower, having lost his wife to cancer seven years ago. When I asked if he would ever remarry, he said no. He was content being single, focusing on his daughter, a 42-year-old mother of four, and his son, who had recently smashed his leg in a motorcycle accident in Hungary. We exchanged emails before I returned to the train.

The return journey was uneventful. I attempted to sleep but couldn't, so I listened to the onboard audio about the history of this part of New Zealand and the people who shaped it. By 8:00 p.m., I was back at Eliza's Manor, exhausted and ready to crash for the night.

Standing next to a Glenorchy Air 9-seater Kodiak plane just after landing in Queenstown from Milford Sound, after a 45-minute flight over the Southern Alps

CHAPTER 12

Queenstown
1ˢᵗ – 3ʳᵈ May

On Wednesday, I woke up at 6:30 a.m., ready for the long drive to Queenstown. By 7:15 a.m., I had loaded my suitcase into my Mitsubishi Outlander and returned inside for breakfast: orange juice, two fried eggs, sourdough bread, three strips of manuka-smoked bacon, and a long black. By 8:00 a.m., I was on the road, my Outlander rolling out of Eliza's Manor's driveway. According to Google Maps, the journey to Queenstown was estimated at six hours and 10 minutes—but with three or four planned stops, I knew there was little chance of keeping to that timeline.

My first stop was at 10:00 a.m. at Farm Shop in Geraldine, about 140 kilometers south of Christchurch. It had been drizzling since I left, and I had hoped that once I got out of Canterbury District, the rain would ease up. It didn't. My second stop was at Lake Tekapo (not "Take a Poo"), where I visited the Church of the Good Shepherd, a stone church built in 1936, perched over the lake. An idyllic place to pray, no doubt, but the doors were locked. After taking several photos, I drove into town for a light lunch. By now, it was almost 1:00 p.m., and the rain still hadn't let up. Most restaurants were closed except for a Chinese restaurant and McKenzie's Café Bar Grill. I chose the latter and ordered a Caesar salad with grilled chicken and a ginger beer. After using the restroom, I accidentally exited into the Chinese restaurant next door and had to backtrack to McKenzie's. I couldn't be certain, but I suspected both places were owned by the same people.

Leaving Lake Tekapo, I continued on Route 8, passing another striking ice-blue lake—Lake Pukaki—which stretched for miles. Further south, I stopped in Omarama for a small cappuccino and a caramel slice. The café staff warned me about the challenging, winding mountain roads ahead near Lindis Pass and again after Cromwell.

Heading south on State Highway 8, I felt like I was traveling through time. The long, straight road out of Omarama led to rolling hills beyond a vast, barren landscape. This was the southern end of the Mackenzie country before the ascent into the distinctive geology of Lindis Pass. Anna Harper had described the landscape here as deeply spiritual, and I now understood why. The arid mountains dwarfed the Judean hills of the Holy Land. There was little greenery—just desert shrubs. The desert strips everything away, leaving only what is essential. In a sense, that is what retirement should do for us so that we can open up to new beginnings, new opportunities.

The next challenge came after Lake Dunstan and Cromwell, a beautiful town where I stopped to refuel—at BP, regrettably, as I generally avoid them due to their disgraceful support of Azerbaijan's dictator, Ilham Aliyev, and his ethnic cleansing of Armenians from Nagorno-Karabakh in 2023. The ascent began at Kawarau on Route 6, winding through Kawarau Gorge and past the Goldfields Mining Centre.

Hairpin bends overlooked deep gorges, their rocks blanketed in autumn hues, and at the bottom, as always, were the ice-blue rushing waters that had captivated me throughout this journey. This delicious torture lasted about 30 minutes. By the time I reached Gibbston, the worst was behind me. Another half-hour later, I entered Queenstown (population: 29,000) and soon pulled up outside the lobby of The Rees Hotel, my new home base. A journey that should have taken six hours had stretched into nine, from 8:00 a.m. to 5:00 p.m., covering nearly 500 kilometers.

Built into the side of a mountain with sweeping views of the lake, the hotel exuded luxury. After checking in and taking a shower, I went down to the restaurant, where I was seated by a window facing the lake. I had a light dinner paired with a lovely local red wine, then returned to my room to journal before calling it an early night.

On Thursday, my alarm went off at 5:30 a.m. I had to be ready for my Milford Sound tour, with a minivan picking me up at 6:35 a.m. at a bus stop opposite The Rees Hotel. Right on time, a Mercedes-Benz minivan arrived. I was the second-to-last pickup. As I settled in, I was informed that the lunch selection consisted of a chicken sandwich or ... a chicken sandwich.

The driver introduced himself as Graham, a Kiwi born in Invercargill, the southernmost city on the South Island. He had been a farmer before transitioning to a career as a tour guide. Married with two sons, he had a warm, engaging presence. He asked each of us to introduce ourselves, which we did. After 50 minutes, we stopped at a roadside food truck for coffee. By 9:00 a.m., we had another stop for breakfast and a bathroom break in Te Anau, pronounced "Tianoo." We took scenic photos at the Te Anau harbor before entering New Zealand's largest national park, Fiordland National Park.

As we drove, Graham shared that the most common trees in New Zealand are red and silver beech, which thrive on the granite mountains. The way they grow is fascinating. A few birch trees dig deep roots, and the rest of the trees in the forest attach themselves to those strong anchors, creating a vast, interconnected network. However, this also has a downside—when an avalanche strikes, entire sections of forest can come crashing down, scarring the mountainside.

We stopped a little further at the Maraoa Waimea ward to catch a glimpse of the Mirror Lakes, which were truly magical. Continuing, we approached the Homer Tunnel, built through the shortest point in the granite mountain range. The tunnel slopes downward at a steep incline—1 meter for every 10—over a distance of 1.8 miles. Constructed during the Great Depression in the 1930s, it took decades to complete. We made additional stops at another mirror lake, the massive waterfall at Falls Creek, and the fast-moving Hollyford River at Whakatipu—pronounced "Fuckatipu" in Māori, which elicited a chuckle from the group.

Soon after, we arrived at Milford Sound (population: 120), which Graham informed us should technically be called Milford Fjord, as sounds are formed by the flooding of river valleys, whereas fjords are created by glacial flooding.

Graham handed out our tickets for the Milford Sound boat trip along with our lunch bags, and we boarded the *Cruise Milford* vessel for a two-hour journey through the fjord. The scenery was spectacular—majestic granite mountains, waterfalls cascading from great heights, and the striking Stirling Falls. The highest permanent waterfall, Lady Bowen Falls, also provides electricity to the town.

Graham presented us with the option to fly back to Queenstown for aerial views of the glaciers. The flight would take just

45 minutes instead of five hours and cost NZ$439. I seized this once-in-a-lifetime opportunity, unwilling to repeat my regret over missing the flight over the Great Barrier Reef. Our pilot, Logan, arranged our transport to Milford Sound Airport, where we boarded a nine-seater Kodiak, a single-engine plane. For 45 glorious minutes, we soared over granite peaks, ice-blue lakes, winding rivers, and breathtaking glaciers of the Southern Alps. It was like flying over Switzerland. The experience was unforgettable—one I hope I will remember even if I live long enough to experience dementia.

On Friday, I was up at 7:00 a.m.—washed, dressed, packed, and down for breakfast by 7:30 a.m. Back in my room by 8:00 a.m., I took some time to journal. I came across a quote on Instagram that resonated deeply: "Be willing to wait for the blessings you deserve. Patience is your greatest lesson. Don't be discouraged. Trust the uncertainty and give yourself time to grow. Don't quit when it gets hard. What's on the other side of the wait will blow you away." It was exactly what I needed to read that morning—an injection of joy.

Lunch today was with Jenny and Graham McDougall, who had invited me out. Over the phone, Graham suggested we meet at Ayrburn in Arrowtown (population: 3,060), about 15 minutes from Queenstown. One of the premier food and wine destinations on the South Island, Ayrburn was a private estate reminiscent of Daylesford in Gloucestershire, England, with an array of restaurants and specialty shops.

We met for lunch and enjoyed grilled kingfish with carrots and roasted potatoes—it was delicious and perfectly complemented by a crisp white wine from France.

After lunch, I drove my Outlander to Avis/Budget at Queenstown Airport to return my car before 3:00 p.m. From there, I walked to the domestic terminal, checked in my luggage, passed through security, and waited in the departure lounge for my flight to Auckland. I would spend the night at a hotel near the airport before my 6:00 a.m. flight to Brisbane, with a 10:00 a.m. connection to Tokyo.

On Saturday morning, I woke at 2:00 a.m. at the Sudima Hotel near Auckland Airport. For some reason, I had been given a hotel suite—luxurious, yet a bit wasted, as I would be there for less than five hours. A driver had been arranged to pick me up at 3:15 a.m., but he didn't arrive until 3:45 a.m. I remained Zen, refusing to let it frustrate me. By the time I got through ticketing and baggage drop-off, it was exactly 4:30 a.m.—just as security and customs were opening.

I slept through most of the three-hour flight from Auckland to Brisbane. At one point, I noticed an elegant woman in her sixties seated a few rows away, rummaging through her hand luggage. Eventually, she pulled out a red apple and ate it—likely to avoid Australia's notoriously strict customs, known for harsh penalties, including fines, jail, or deportation.

Later, while waiting at the international lounge's food and drink counter, I ran into her and her partner again. We struck up a conversation. Her name was Coralie, a South African, and her partner, Chris, was a Kiwi. They had met on Tinder, hit it off, and before the pandemic, Chris had flown to South Africa to visit her, staying for six months. Now, they split their time between South Africa and New Zealand, six months in each country.

Before boarding my Qantas flight to Tokyo, I called my daughter Elizabeth on WhatsApp and had a brief five-minute chat.

45 days completed.

35 days remaining.

PART 4

JAPAN

"It is impossible to remain indifferent to
Japanese culture.
It is a different civilization where all you
have learnt must be forgotten.
It is a great intellectual challenge and a gorgeous
sensual experience."

Alain Ducasse
The world's most decorated chef

Japan

- Kanazawa
- Kyoto
- Osaka
- Hiroshima
- Tokyo
- Mt. Fuji
- Tsumago
- Mt. Koya

CHAPTER 13

Tokyo
4th – 7th May

I arrived on Saturday evening at 6:45 p.m. at Narita International Airport, where I was met by Koharu, a Japanese representative from the local agency handling my travel arrangements. She went through all the pre-booked rail tickets I would need for the next three weeks in Japan and handed them over to me. She then escorted me to a private taxi, which took me to Hotel Gracery in Ginza.

On Sunday, I woke up at 6:00 a.m. and stayed in bed for half an hour before getting up to wash, dress, and head downstairs for breakfast. Japanese breakfasts are a unique experience, featuring fish, chicken, meats, and pickled vegetables—none of which resonate with me in the morning. Observing other guests, I saw them taking large white trays and filling the small partitions with a selection of items from the buffet. Following their lead, I chose pineapple, melon, two boiled eggs, cold meats, square bacon, two small croissants, a sesame roll, and a small bowl of yogurt with blueberry jam. I also drank two cups of black coffee.

At around 8:30 a.m., I went down to reception to use the safe deposit, as the one in my room wasn't working. Shortly after, I met my guide and interpreter, Keiichi Tamura, who went by Kei. He took me to a local teahouse, where he spent about 45 minutes explaining how Tokyo's railway and subway networks operate in the world's most populated city, with 14 million people. We then walked to Shinbashi Station, an eight-minute walk from my hotel, where, in a few days, I would take the JR Yamanote Line to Shinagawa Station to board the Shinkansen, or bullet train, to my next destination, Nagoya.

Kei handed me an IC travel card—like an Oyster card in London—and loaded it with ¥1,000, about US$7 or £5. I then followed him onto a subway train to Shiodome, and we walked to Hama-rikyu Gardens, a beautiful green space in Tokyo. Originally a family garden for the Tokugawa Shogunate, it also functioned as an outer fort for Edo Castle and retains a tidal seawater pond fed from the local bay. Since its establishment in 1654, it had served various shoguns until the Meiji Restoration, when it became a detached palace for the Imperial family and was renamed Hama-rikyu Gardens. In 1945, the Imperial family donated the garden to the city of Tokyo, and after restoration, it was opened to the public the following year.

Kei then took me to one of the reconstructed *ochayas* (teahouses) on an island in the middle of a lake within the gardens. Various shoguns had once enjoyed tea here, and now, so did we. We sipped *matcha* (powdered green tea) with a traditional sweet. As we walked through the gardens, Kei pointed out plum trees, peach blossoms, magnolias, and cherry blossoms—though no longer in season. He explained that in Japan, *sakura* (cherry blossoms) are revered not only for their fleeting beauty but also for the comfort and promise they bring in their return each year.

From there, we took the subway to the outer gardens of the Imperial Palace—a long, hot walk in the midday sun.

Eventually, we made our way back through the Marunouchi district, lined with high-end shops much like Bond Street in London or Fifth Avenue in New York. Kei then walked me back to my hotel, where we parted ways.

Back in my room, I freshened up and changed into a clean shirt before my meeting with Altair (Steven) Shyam. A renowned shaman, Altair had been recommended to me by my friend Raquel Spring, a fourth-generation astrologer in Sedona, Arizona. She believed we would get along well. I waited outside the hotel entrance until Altair approached. He recognized me from the photo on my website. We went to a nearby restaurant, where, over a salad lunch, we exchanged stories about our lives. I told him about my journey and the sense of being in a liminal space, embracing uncertainty about my next steps. His story fascinated me.

Given his shamanic background, I asked about his ancestry and whether he had any Māori heritage. He shared that his lineage was Māori and English on his father's side and Māori, French, and Irish on his mother's. His grandmother had belonged to a Māori royal family, but her entire tribe in Christchurch had been massacred by a Māori tribe from Wellington. At 15, his mother was sent to live with an aunt in Nelson, on the South Island. A Māori elder had once told her she would have two sons and two daughters, and that her eldest—Altair—would become a monk. Fearing that prophecy, she never spoke of it to him until just months before she passed away.

Prior to his current Japanese wife, Altair had two previous partners and fathered five children. His eldest is 34, and his youngest daughter, whom he had with his current wife—17 years his junior—is nine. I enjoyed my time with Altair, and he shared two pieces of valuable advice. First, always live in the present moment. Second, think back to a time when you were in a state of love, joy, and flow, and practice that feeling at every opportunity or challenge. No one can give us that sense of love, joy, and flow—it must come from within. I could have spoken with him for hours, and I'm deeply grateful to have met him.

During our conversation, Altair mentioned that one of his aunts, a nun in Australia, had introduced him to the Christian concept of the Cloud of Unknowing (also the title of a book I've read and still have on my Kindle). This idea has always fascinated me, as it acknowledges an element of surprise and mystery in life that is beyond our control. Upon returning to my room, I revisited the book with fresh eyes. It occurred to me that retirement places one in a liminal space—a transition between what was and what will be. The book suggests that to know God, one must have the courage to surrender the mind and ego to the realm of unknowing. In short, "Let go and let God."

The book advises the student to seek God not through knowledge and intellect but through deep contemplation, driven by love and free of thought. This is achieved by casting all distractions under a "cloud of forgetting" and piercing God's "cloud of unknowing" with a dart of longing love from the heart. Though the author remains anonymous, the theme of the cloud appeared earlier in *The Confessions of St. Augustine*, written in 398 A.D. Fast-forward to retirement—this phase of life is like a chrysalis, a crisis (a turning point), a painful transformation, or a cloud of unknowing. Our instinct is fight or flight. Instead, I remind myself to sit with the fear and explore the infinite possibilities that lie ahead—if only I have the courage to do so.

On Monday, I woke up at 5:00 a.m. and couldn't go back to sleep, so I checked my itinerary for the next few days. I had planned to visit the Tokyo Museum, but this week is Japan's Golden Week, and today is Children's Day, meaning most public institutions were closed. However, shrines remained open, so I decided to visit Sensō-ji Temple in the Asakusa district.

After breakfast, just after 8:00 a.m., I made my way to the Tokyo subway and took the Orange Line G9 from Ginza to Asakusa. About 200 meters from the station stands Japan's oldest Buddhist temple, a colorful and popular site said to have been built in 628 A.D. I walked around, taking in both the architecture and the people. What struck me was the juxtaposition of faith and commerce—devotees praying and making offerings while merchants and priests conducted a roaring trade. Worshippers wrote a single wish on a plywood plaque and paid for the privilege. Naturally, many had multiple wishes, so the money flowed steadily into the temple. Having been raised Catholic, I recognized the practice, but I had to admire the efficiency of Buddhist fundraising—nothing in life is free. We pay for our priests, ministers, and rabbis to bless us, marry us, and bury us.

Emerging from the subway near my hotel, I walked a few blocks using Google Maps to reach Mitsukoshi, one of Tokyo's top department stores. I had an idea stuck in my head—I wanted a kimono. However, nothing they had appealed to me, so I searched for a specialist kimono shop and found Tansuya Ginzaten, not far from where I was. An elderly Japanese lady kindly assisted me, but I was disappointed again—most of the kimonos were either too dark or too garish.

Leaving empty-handed and disappointed, I looked for a good ramen spot and found Ginza Kagari Soba at the top of a list of the best ramen places in the area. I queued up, and when I was finally seated, I ordered chicken ramen noodles with spring onions, soy sauce, and ginger paste, paired with a Kirin beer. The broth was delicious—light and deeply satisfying.

Back in my hotel room at 1:30 p.m., I freshened up and decided to visit the famous Meiji Jingu (Meiji Shrine). This Shinto shrine is set within a vast 70-hectare man-made forest in southwest Tokyo. It was established in 1920 to commemorate Emperor Meiji (1852–1912) and Empress Shōken (1850–1914) following their deaths. Thanks to the donation of 100,000 trees from across Japan and the voluntary efforts of young people, the forest was designed to be self-regenerating, planned by forestry experts with a vision for the next 100 years. However, most of the shrine complex was destroyed during the air raids of World War II in 1945. Fortunately, the forest survived, and the shrine was reconstructed in 1958 with the support of the public, restoring it to its original grandeur. Emperor Meiji ushered Japan into modernity with the Meiji Restoration of 1868, ending 200 years of isolationist policy. This era also marked the dissolution of the feudal shogunate and the samurai class—noble warrior monks who had served the emperor. The Meiji period introduced modernization and scientific advancements to Japan, which is why the emperor and empress are so revered.

Upon returning to the hotel, I asked the front desk to send my suitcase by rail to my next hotel in Tsumago. In Japan, rail travel is the ideal and most economical way to explore the country. The rail system is so punctual it undoubtedly rivals the Swiss. One particularly convenient service allows travelers to dispatch their luggage to their next destination ahead of time, freeing them to sightsee unburdened. The cost is a reasonable $15. The front desk informed me they could arrange this for tomorrow but could only accept cash, which I didn't have. So, I rushed to the nearest department store, Matsuya, before closing time, took the elevator up to the eighth floor where the accounts department was located, and exchanged a US$100 bill for about ¥15,000. In the past, such an inconvenience would have agitated me, but no longer—I took deep breaths and stayed Zen. I was ready for my journey into the Japanese countryside.

On Tuesday, after breakfast around 8:00 a.m., I went to the concierge, submitted my completed luggage form, and made the cash payment to have my suitcase delivered to Fukinomori Ryokan, a traditional Japanese inn near Tsumago. I walked to Shinbashi Station to catch my train to Shinagawa, four stops away on the JR Line, but not before adding another ¥1,000 to my IC card. I arrived an hour early for my 11:00 a.m. departure, so I stopped at a café and ordered an Americano and a donut—no judgment. My journey today involved three trains. First, the 11:07 a.m. Shinkansen (bullet train) to Nagoya, a 90-minute ride. At Nagoya, I transferred to an express train to Nakatsugawa, a 50-minute journey. From there, I boarded a local train to Nagiso, an 18-minute ride.

CHAPTER 14

Tsumago and the Nakasendō Trail
7th – 9th May

On arriving in Nagiso (population: 4,111), I waited half an hour for the 3:00 p.m. shuttle bus to my hotel, Fukinomori. I bet you're thinking what I was thinking—it sounds like "Fuckin' Omori," right? Oh my, this hotel is a jewel of Japanese culture. My room looked like a scene from *The Last Samurai*, with its light-colored wood-paneled sliding doors. The view from my window was spiritual: rain pouring down on a forest of trees covering the mountains, all hidden by mist.

By the time I settled into my room, Zuiou, in the Sunrise building, it was past 4:00 p.m. I dressed in the hotel *yukata* (a casual, shorter Japanese kimono) and slippers and made my way downstairs to the onsen (Japanese hot springs). This was my first time experiencing an onsen, which is segregated for men and women because full nudity is required. I was nervous because I have tattoos on my arms: an Aztec eagle on my left and the symbol of Aquarius (living waters) on my right. In Japan, tattoos are socially frowned upon and often associated with the criminal underworld. When I entered the onsen, two elderly Japanese men were already sitting in it. I slowly sank into the hot springs, which were so hot at first that I felt my skin was being peeled off. After a few minutes, though, the heat became bearable, even pleasant. Twenty minutes later, I got up and went to the adjacent area, where I sat on a stool and showered myself with a handheld shower, as is the custom. When I struggled to open my locker, one of the elderly men kindly helped me. I thoroughly enjoyed my onsen experience and felt unusually relaxed and uplifted.

Upstairs in the lounge, I met two Caucasian women dressed in elegant, floral-patterned kimonos, adorned with shades of pink and lavender. I introduced myself, and they turned out to be Aussies from New South Wales. We had tea and chatted before parting ways. I was booked for dinner at 6:30 p.m., so I proceeded to the restaurant, where I was ushered into a small, wood-paneled private and personal dining room. The table and seat were legless, and sitting down wasn't comfortable at first—my pelvis protested loudly before settling. My dinner was a feast of many small dishes. For appetizers, I had apple wine, pork with yuzu pepper sauce, Kagome spring vegetables with sesame sauce, *zuiki* (pickled taro stems), bamboo shoots with vinegar miso, and smelt, a tiny fish. The main course featured single servings: a chicken hotpot, horse sashimi (a local delicacy), *sansai soba* (handmade with herbs), tempura snow trout, and mushroom rice with pickles. For dessert, I had white grape sorbet washed down with hot saké.

As I ate, I reflected on why obesity seems rare in Japan. Perhaps it's because the Japanese see abundance and variety in their meals, allowing their senses to dictate when they've had enough. They also follow the Confucian-inspired adage *hara hachi bu*—a reminder to stop eating when their stomachs are 80 percent full. Such wise advice!

The next morning, I went down to breakfast at 8:00 a.m. Fukinomori served a traditional Japanese breakfast in my private dining room, where I pretended to myself that I was a samurai. The meal included rice, a salad bowl, and a plate of three types of fish: a white fish, a yellow fish, and a breaded fish, alongside a mini charcoal oven for cooking. There was also a small solo stove with a flame, a flat pan, one egg, and three pieces of bacon. I cooked the fish and eggs with enthusiasm.

At 9:50 a.m., I took the hotel shuttle bus to Tsumago with a group from our hotel, including the two Aussie women. We were dropped off at a local bus stop, where we boarded a bus to Magome-juku (population in the low hundreds). We paid ¥600 ($4) in cash to the driver upon exiting. Our plan was to hike an 8.5-kilometer stretch of the historic Nakasendō Trail, part of the original highway that once connected Kyoto and Tokyo. This trail is a spiritual journey, akin to Spain's Camino de Santiago, where samurai and pilgrims once walked roughly 540 kilometers. Known as the journey to the heart of Japan, it winds through 69 post towns, linking Kyoto, Japan's ancient capital, to Tokyo, its modern counterpart.

The cobblestone roads of the historic Nakasendō Route and the quaint Edo-period (1603–1868) post towns of the Kiso Valley make you feel as though you've stepped back in time to the age of the samurai. The Nakasendō, literally the "central mountain route," was a mountainous inland path that once connected Kyoto to Edo (present-day Tokyo) during the Edo period. Most of the original Nakasendō Route has been lost to time or transformed into modern roads and highways.

Today, I was going to experience the best-preserved and most beautiful portion of the Nakasendō Trail: the stretch from Magome-juku to Tsumago-juku, which winds through the Kiso Valley in Nagano Prefecture. When the bus dropped us off at the Magome bus stop, I wasn't initially impressed. But as I began to climb the steep, stone-built path, lined with shops on both sides and a running stream dotted with windmills, I understood why this is called the prettiest village in Japan. Walking up the cobblestone path, a sign for the Tōson Memorial Museum caught my attention. The famous Japanese poet and writer Shimazaki Tōson (1872–1943) was born here, and many of his novels are set in this area. As a fellow writer, I felt drawn to visit his museum. Intrigued, I paid ¥500 to enter. Much of the material wasn't in English, so I ended up watching a 45-minute video in Japanese with English subtitles. Tōson published several collections of poems and novels, and in 1935, he became the first chairman of the Japan PEN Club. In 1947, three years after his death, the original Tōson Memorial Museum was built by the people of Magome in his honor.

Back on the trail, I noticed that many of my hotel guests had already moved on. I was happy to be on my own. I've grown fond of my solitude, my own company, especially on walks like this one.

The first two miles were steep, and along the way, I came across an Aussie couple from Canberra. They were nice enough but very stiff, unlike the two Aussie women from my hotel, whose company was fun until they wanted to be on their own. I also met a young German couple with whom I did not feel a connection, and another young couple, German speakers from South Tyrol in northern Italy, who were full of energy. The landscape was breathtaking, and I marveled at the lush hues of green that washed over my eyes, as well as the refreshing waters of the small streams that appeared here and there. I arrived at the first lunch canteen, where I noticed three young men speaking German and eating a pot of soba noodles with spring onions. I raised my eyebrows in approval at their plates, and they invited me to join them, which I did. The food was great, and so was the conversation, but we all had to move on. They had a train to catch, and I still had five miles to go—it was already 12:45 p.m.

Without further distraction, I focused on my forest bathing, breathing in the delicious oxygen and letting my eyes feast on the delightful waterfalls that seemed to appear at every turn. I took photos to capture the sights, but more importantly, I absorbed the energy into my core. I finally reached the bus stop at 3:00 p.m. and was back in my hotel room 30 minutes later. My bag had arrived from Tokyo. I put on my *yukata* and went downstairs for my onsen and sauna, after which I felt a sensation that my skin was alive and rejuvenated. I suspect I'll sleep like a baby tonight.

Sitting in the onsen, I reflected on my walk earlier that day, and it dawned on me that nature is chaotic and messy. I pictured the broken, felled trees covering the ground and the streams. How strange that we try to keep our lives tidy, when our lives are messy—just like a forest. And there's nothing wrong with that. We just must learn to accept it. It was a wonderful insight.

On Thursday, I woke up at 6:30 a.m. and went down for breakfast—another Japanese breakfast. It's hard to face a plate of fish, rice, pickles, miso soup, and mushrooms in the morning. I miss my simple breakfasts. Also, I'm not partial to sitting on the floor in a chair with no legs at a low table. My legs were going numb!

My luggage, which I dropped at the front desk, was shortly due to be picked up for delivery to my next hotel in Kanazawa. In the meantime, I made my way to the shuttle at 9:45 a.m. to go to Nagiso Station, where I would catch the 11:00 a.m. express train headed to Kanazawa via Nagano, with a one-hour layover. At Nagano, I managed to eat a sandwich and drink a coffee before boarding the Shinkansen Hakutaka No. 563 to Kanazawa.

Standing with Samurai descendant, historian,
and swordsman, Masahisa Shijiyama,
in his studio in Kanazawa, after a brief sword-fighting session.

CHAPTER 15

Kanazawa
9th – 12th May

About 80 minutes later, my train arrived in Kanazawa (population: 465,699). After consulting the information desk, I took bus number 5 to Ōmichō Market, where I enjoyed four succulent pieces of wagyu beef on a skewer, cooked in front of me and served with wasabi sauce. I then boarded the Orange Loop bus, headed to the rail station, and, after some struggle despite using my Google apps, I found the shuttle bus to my new hotel: Sainoniwa. After checking into my room and settling in, I went to a nearby soba noodle house called Sobadokoro Yabu for dinner.

On Friday, I woke up at 5:30 a.m. I reviewed my schedule for the next few days and noted that tomorrow I had a special four-hour samurai tour guide scheduled. I decided on three sites to visit today: Kenroku-en Gardens, Kanazawa Castle Park, and the D.T. Suzuki Museum. On a map of Kanazawa, Kenroku-en Gardens and Kanazawa Castle Park sit at the city's center, just as they are central to its history.

My first visit was to Kenroku-en Gardens, whose name means "Garden of the Six Attributes" in Japanese. It's considered a classic because it combines all six elements of excellence—something nearly impossible, according to their brochure. The six elements are spaciousness, artificiality, water features, seclusion, antiquity, and panoramas.

The garden has evolved over time but was originally built in 1676 by the fifth lord of the Kaga Domain, Maeda Tsunanori. After the abolition of the feudal domains, Kenroku-en Gardens was opened to the public in 1874. It features an island, a bridge, a teahouse, several ponds, waterfalls, streams, pines, plum groves, and the oldest fountain in Japan. Back in 1632, after a large fire at the castle, the lord of the domain had a channel built from 11 kilometers upstream of the Sai River along the slope of the plateau. To this day, the channel brings clean water to Kenroku-en Gardens, the castle, and the city.

My second visit was to Kanazawa Castle and Park, just across the road from Kenroku-en Gardens. The size of the castle walls is so vast that it dwarfs those of any castle in Europe. The grey stone walls are imposing and intimidating. There's an outer wall and an inner wall, with gates placed at different angles to force potential invaders to expose themselves to attacks from three directions—a highly effective defensive configuration. The castle was originally constructed in the late 16th century. The interior buildings, made entirely of wood, were destroyed by fire because of lightning and reconstructed in 1788, remaining intact to this day. The construction of the joints is intricate and sophisticated, interlaced to create extra strength. The roof was made of wood and covered with lead tiles about two millimeters thick. Why lead? The Kaga region had an abundance of it, and during wartime, it could be melted down to make bullets. Lastly, over 200 symbols are carved into the castle walls. One theory suggests they may have been used to identify where the stones were quarried.

The third visit was to the D.T. Suzuki Museum, a 10-minute ride on the Orange Loop bus and a short walk away. Anna Harper in New Zealand had highly recommended it. Suzuki was a world-renowned Buddhist philosopher, a native of Kanazawa, who studied philosophy at Tokyo University and worked as an editor in Illinois for 11 years. While there, he married Beatrice Erskine Lane, an American theosophist. When they returned to Japan, they founded the Eastern Buddhist Society. Suzuki eventually became a professor at Tokyo University and frequently lectured at leading universities in the US and Europe.

The museum is minimalist and Zen, featuring stone, water, and vegetation. Inside, there's an exhibition space about Suzuki, including a surprising photo of him with Martin Heidegger, the German philosopher I had come to learn about a few years earlier. In the learning space, there's a table, chairs, and a library. A beautiful excerpt from Suzuki's book *Zen and the Love of Nature* was displayed—an essay titled "Appreciate the Benefits of Nature." Sadly, photos weren't allowed, so I couldn't capture it. I tried searching for it online later but had little success. Finally, there's a contemplative space with three open portals overlooking a shallow pool, trees, and shrubs from different perspectives. I chose to read three sheets of Suzuki's writings, one for each portal, and meditated on them. One quote that resonated deeply with me was:

> "*The most effective act is, once the mind is made up, to go on without looking backward.*"

After leaving the museum, I walked for 30 minutes to a department store near Ōmichō Market called M'ZA. I tried on a silk kimono that I liked very much, but it wasn't exactly what I wanted, and it was expensive, so I reluctantly left it behind. Nowadays, no matter how much I desire something, if it doesn't resonate with me, I let it go. Next, I walked into the bar of a small local restaurant nearby, where I enjoyed soba noodles with prawns and pork.

I needed to rest and recharge, so I returned to my hotel. Slipping into the hotel *yukata*, I headed to the onsen. As I lay immersed in the hot spring waters, I contemplated the water garden at the Suzuki Museum and reflected on the messages in Suzuki's essays. It dawned on me that the phrase "let go and let God" does not mean we must surrender our longing for a love that is deeply spiritual, profoundly psychic and wholly devotional. That is the love I am seeking. I believe in this love. What or who it is I do not yet know. I like to think I possess a quiet knowing, but I cannot be certain until it makes itself known. I have faith, and I choose to remain in this state of unknowing—this cloud of unknowing—which feels like a sacred place of co-creation. Just like a sailboat must push its rudder in the opposite direction to reach its destination, I too must now steer my vessel against the direction of my desires. I need to get out of my own way. I must dive deeper to uncover what my heart truly longs for. My voice is meant to be heard, and my hidden gift is ready to emerge. I am an eagle dancer—and I must dance. My heart is calling, and I am ready to respond.

On Saturday morning, after breakfast, I waited in the lobby at 9:15 a.m. for my guide and interpreter for the half-day samurai history tour. A small woman approached me and introduced herself as Ms. Kazu Takatsuka. She had a taxi waiting outside to take us to a teashop in the Yayoi district, about five kilometers away. We arrived in about 15 minutes, and upon entering the teashop, a young lady offered us a cup of green tea. I didn't ask, nor was I told, what we were doing there. This was unusual for me—not that I was shy or uninterested, but I wanted things to unfold naturally. After about 10 minutes, a slender man with a full head of grey hair and glasses introduced himself as Mr. Masahisa Shijiyama, or Masa for short. Masa was the president of his company and the shop owner. He led us to his office at the back of the teashop. I would later learn that his family business specializes in fermented foods, with various shops, including one at Kanazawa Station. In his hand, Masa held a long, cylindrical blue tube. He pulled out a scroll from inside it and unfurled it on the table to show me his family's lineage, tracing all the way back to 1603, when the shogunate of Tokugawa Ieyasu was established.

Tokugawa allowed each *daimyo* (feudal lord) to administer his *han* (feudal domain). In Kanazawa, the feudal lord was Lord Maeda Toshiie. Masa's ancestor served as the eyes and ears of Tokugawa, monitoring Lord Maeda's activities. Fast forward to 1868, with the Meiji Restoration, power returned to the emperor, the feudal system was dismantled, and the samurai class was abolished. Some samurai became policemen, postmen, or even servants, while a few turned to commerce. Masa's wife's family were also former samurai who became merchants. Since her family had no son, Masa took on his wife's family name. On his side of the family, Masa is the middle son, but because his elder brother has no son, Masa inherited all the samurai swords and family regalia. His family crest is three trees, or *mori*. The passion he displayed for his ancestry reminded me of my old school friend Robert Clifford Holmes, who traced his lineage back to 1066 and William the Conqueror.

In some ways, I find that honoring tradition is a beautiful act, and it should be appreciated without mortgaging our present or future. I think both British and Japanese traditions overemphasize the past to the detriment of their present and future. The house Masa and his wife live in has been in her family for generations. Masa showed me a framed photograph of his wedding, and I couldn't help but say, "You both look so handsome, but what happened to you?" Seconds later, he broke into laughter once he registered what I had said. He had a good sense of humor. I also discovered that, like me, Masa was born in 1955, and I sensed an immediate connection between us.

Masa shared and displayed his wife's family swords, including a small dagger she wore on their wedding day. Samurai women would use such daggers to kill themselves if their husbands were killed, avoiding the shame of becoming concubines. He then showed me his family's longswords, much heavier and more detailed, all crafted between 500 and 200 years ago. Masa explained the intricacies of master swordsmithing and demonstrated how to carry, unsheathe, use, and resheathe a samurai sword. His wife had prepared a tatami mat, soaked overnight in water to replicate a human body (which is 75% water), and placed it upright on a plinth. Masa unsheathed his sword and cut through the water-laden mat diagonally in three effortless thrusts.

As Masa's wife picked up the cut pieces, I told her I had seen their wedding photograph and commented on how handsome they both looked. I mentioned the small dagger displayed on her wedding dress and asked if she had ever had cause to use it on Masa. Ms. Kazu translated, and after a brief pause, she burst into giggles.

Finally, Masa honored me with a certificate. It was an enjoyable and educational session on samurai history and swords.

Masa left me with the samurai masters' nine rules for success in life. The code of conduct was essentially elaborated by Miyamoto Musashi, a *ronin* warrior who had lost his master. Despite their brevity, the nine rules are a remarkable guide for reflection and decisiveness, demanding understanding and continual practice.

Here they are:

1. Do not think dishonestly. Think honestly and truthfully. Do not harbor sinister designs.
2. The way is in training. One must always continue to train.
3. Become acquainted with every art.
4. Know the way of all professions.
5. Know the difference between loss and gain in worldly matters.
6. Develop intuitive judgment and understanding for everything.
7. Perceive those things which cannot be seen.
8. Pay attention even to trifles.
9. Do nothing which is of no use.

These are timeless rules because humanity is in dire need of people who think correctly—for their own benefit as much as for the benefit of others.

Next, Ms. Kazu took me to the local samurai house of the Nomura family (no relation to the famous Japanese banking family). We explored the various rooms, exhibitions of armor, coins, weapons, and artwork on the doors and nail covers. The house featured a Zen Garden with flowing water and a small waterfall, creating a calming rhythm. The drawing room was made of Japanese cypress wood, with elaborate designs in rosewood and ebony. The sliding doors bore a landscape painted by Sasaki-sensei, a highly ranked artist of the Kanō school.

On Sunday, I woke up at 5:30 a.m. and stayed in bed for an hour. Since I was leaving for Osaka today, I packed my bags and went down for breakfast at 7:00 a.m. I finished in half an hour and returned upstairs to rest before catching the shuttle bus from the hotel at 9:10 a.m. By 9:20 a.m., I was inside Kanazawa Station, heading toward the Shinkansen scheduled to depart at 9:46 a.m. By 12:20 p.m., I arrived at Osaka Station, which was so enormous it dwarfed London's St Pancras.

CHAPTER 16

Osaka
12ᵗʰ – 13ᵗʰ May

Built over Osaka Station are nine floors of shops, cafés, and restaurants. I had a devil of a time getting out of the station—no surprise, given that Osaka (population: 2,592,413) is Japan's third-largest city. It was raining, so I went back inside to wait it out. I found a small restaurant on the top floor and sat down for my usual lunch: miso soup, noodles, and tempura prawns and vegetables.

By 1:00 p.m., I was out and about, looking for Zentis Hotel. My Google Maps was confused because the app couldn't differentiate between pedestrian walkways and overhead paths around the station. Eventually, I met an American couple who, by chance, were also heading to the same hotel. Together, we figured out how to get there. I finally checked into my room, took a shower, and washed and dried my clothes in the hotel's coin laundry while enjoying a drink and a snack. Since my next few stops were short stays, I decided it would be sensible to leave my suitcase at the hotel in Osaka and pick it up the following week when I returned. I packed clothing and toiletries into my backpack and took my suitcase down to the front desk for storage.

That evening, I was set to join a tour called Flavors of Osaka Food, starting at 5:00 p.m. Earlier, while having a snack at the bar, I met two English women from Kent who were talking about a food tour that evening—surprisingly, the same one I was on. One of the women was aloof, and the other seemed miserable, but I wasn't going to let anyone ruin my evening. We ended up sharing a taxi to our meeting point. When we arrived, we tried to split the bill. I wanted to pay with my Caxton multi-currency debit card, while the women wanted to pay in cash. This flustered our taxi driver, who motioned us out of the car and walked us to our meeting point, leaving his engine running and the money on the dashboard. Why didn't he take my card? How could he be so confident his car and money would still be there when he returned? I'm sure he had his reasons, but I was perplexed—and I still don't understand what happened.

At the meeting point, the first to join us were a Swiss couple, Lukas and Barbara from Bern, followed by two more English couples. We chatted and waited at least 30 minutes for our guide. Lukas eventually called his agent in Tokyo to find out what was going on, while the rest of us went to a local bar for a drink. Just as we were about to order, our guide, Hanai, arrived, apologizing profusely. She thought our meeting was at 6:00 p.m. The Japanese word for "sorry" or "pardon" is *sumimasen*, one of my favorite words, which I used frequently because it has magical powers—it always makes Japanese people respond with a smile. Hanai more than made up for the delay that evening. Osaka is the food capital of Japan, much like Lyon is for France and Melbourne for Australia. Our first dégustation was at a restaurant that served wagyu beef over a small personal charcoal oven: short loin, sirloin, and rib, with two different dipping sauces, paired with an ice-cold Kirin beer. It was perfect!

Next, we walked down well-lit alleys to another small restaurant, where we were led to an upstairs room to try *okonomiyaki*, a Japanese pancake made with shredded cabbage, *okonomi* sauce, eggs, green onions, spring onions, and a protein—often pork belly—grilled on a *teppan* or flat-top grill. The name *okonomiyaki* loosely means "as you like." Hanai explained that in Japanese homes, this pancake is often made with leftover foods to economize, much like how pizza became popular in Italy. The famous *puttanesca* (meaning "whore" in Italian) is a similar concept—everything is thrown into it. Our third and final stop was a restaurant serving *kushikatsu*, deep-fried meat, shrimp, and vegetables with a side of soy sauce. The only rule: you can only dip once. I had a chance to speak with Lukas, who had saved the evening by alerting Hanai through his agent. Like many of us, Lukas is navigating a major career transition as a top functionary in the Swiss health sector, so I helped him think and feel his way through it. It was a wonderful evening overall. I returned to the hotel in a taxi shared with the two English women, who had warmed up a bit—no doubt thanks to the alcohol.

CHAPTER 17

Hiroshima and Miyajima
13th – 15th May

On Monday morning, after breakfast, I took a taxi to Shin Osaka to catch my 9:41 a.m. Shinkansen to Hiroshima. I arrived in Hiroshima at 11:00 a.m. and took tram number 2 to Fukuro-machi, from where it was a five-minute walk to the Mitsui Garden Hotel. Since check-in was at 3:00 p.m., I left my backpack at the hotel and headed to the Hiroshima Peace Memorial Museum.

Hiroshima, meaning "broad island" in Japanese, is the country's 11th-largest city, with a current population of just under 1.2 million. In 1942, the population was just under 420,000, but it dropped to 137,000 after the atomic bomb. Remarkably, Hiroshima not only survived the bomb but continues to grow and thrive. Historically, it was a commercial port city on Hiroshima Bay, with a strong military and industrial base. The decision by the US to drop the atomic bomb on Hiroshima was due to its military significance.

The Peace Memorial Museum opened in August 1955, a decade after the bomb was dropped. The permanent exhibition is divided into six areas: Hiroshima before the bombing; the devastation and damage on August 6, 1945; victims and survivors; the construction of the peace memorial; the dangers of nuclear weapons; and the reconstruction of Hiroshima. Adjacent to the main building is the Peace Memorial Hall, opened in 2002, which hosts special exhibitions, a water fountain, a slope to the Hall of Remembrance, a victims' information area, and a library.

On August 6, 1945, at 8:15 a.m., an American B-29 bomber dropped the world's first deployed atomic bomb, known as "Little Boy," on Hiroshima. In the early 1990s, while working on my master's degree in journalism at New York University, I read John Hersey's book *Hiroshima*, which affected me deeply. Yet, nothing compares to visiting this memorial and witnessing the impact it had on the people of this city. The human mind struggles to comprehend such carnage. Yes, 80,000 people were incinerated immediately, and another 60,000 suffered illnesses for years or decades. The horror makes Dante's *Inferno* seem almost palatable. It wasn't just the burns, blisters, and sheets of burnt skin hanging like rags from the victims. The personal stories of men, women, and children were harrowing. I could only read a few dozen before feeling nauseous and overwhelmed by the sheer scale of the suffering.

My mind began to compare it to the Jewish Shoah or the Armenian Genocide. The question isn't which was worse in terms of lives lost, but rather, how can human beings do this to each other? All religions teach that life is about suffering and redemption. Even love involves suffering. Yet, emotionally, my heart breaks at the sheer scale of humanity's suffering. All I can do is keep the light of my candle flickering.

A few stories touched me deeply. The first were the quotes from victims etched on a plaque: "It hurts." "Hurts." "Hot." "Water." "Help." "Mother." "I don't want to die." "How could this have happened to me?" "My son, where are you?" "I'm sorry, I cannot save you." Each of those who perished, as well as those who survived, cried out from the depths of their hearts.

The second is the spirit of Hiroshima: "No one else should suffer as we have." I think of all the retirees who have faded into the fog of dementia because they stopped truly living. What a tragic loss—for themselves, their families, and for humanity. I came to Hiroshima—or perhaps it called to me—because I wanted to witness how a city that was once incinerated could rise again. I wanted to hold it up as a living example of what "liminal space" is, or what it means to dwell in the "cloud of unknowing." How do we move from devastation to renewal? How do we step from retirement into a new beginning? Think of how the crucible of suffering on Robben Island transformed Nelson Mandela from a defiant young lawyer and activist into a wise and humble leader.

But here in Hiroshima, the heartrending message of the *hibakusha* (the surviving victims of the atomic bomb) resonates—"No one else should suffer as we have"—forged in the cauldron of suffering and sorrow, transcending hatred and rejection. Its spirit of generosity and love for humanity directs its focus to the future of humankind. In response to the *hibakusha*'s appeal, the epitaph on the cenotaph for the A-bomb victims reads, "Let all the souls here rest in peace, for we shall not repeat this evil." These words express the spirit of Hiroshima, pursuing harmony and prosperity for all and yearning for genuine and lasting world peace.

The third story that touched me was in the temporary exhibition at the Peace Memorial Hall, which began on March 1, 2024, and will run for 12 months. It tells the story of the Akatsuki Corps, the boy soldiers, aged 15 to 19, of the Suicide Attack Squad of Hiroshima. They joined believing they were saving Japan and were trained for suicide missions on small plywood boats, just under six meters long, carrying depth charges. Their objective was to attack enemy (US) ships at night at a 45-degree angle to sink them. This secret operation, known as Maru-Re, collapsed on August 6, 1945, when the bomb fell. Their commander ordered the boy soldiers to aid and care for the victims and burn corpses to prevent disease.

The exhibition explores the mindset of these young soldiers. I watched a video documentary that featured the testimonies of several former soldiers—now frail, elderly men. One story moved me deeply. A young soldier had encountered a distraught mother cradling her lifeless child, pleading with him, "Please take me back to Nara." As it happened, the soldier was also from Nara, a suburb of Osaka, and he felt an immediate connection. He told the mother that her child had died—and what's more, she would not be allowed to travel on a train with a deceased infant. He sought permission from his commanding officer to cremate the child's body and return the ashes to the mother in an urn. Permission was granted, but just as he was about to proceed, he realized he felt uneasy with her standing there watching. He explained how he felt and asked her to come back in a few hours. When she returned, he gave her the urn and accompanied her to the train station. Choking up, he recalled how the memory of that day had stayed with him ever since. Many years later, the mother tracked him down and visited his family home. He was not there, so she spoke with his father instead. She told him she had remarried and had children but had never forgotten the young soldier's act of compassion. She wanted to express her thanks. When the soldier returned home, his father relayed the message—but he was disappointed that she hadn't left her address, and that his father hadn't thought to ask. It troubled him deeply, because he too had long wanted to thank her. A remarkable story—though a bittersweet ending.

That evening, I had dinner at a local restaurant and sat at the bar. Earlier, I had reflected on how most restaurants in Japan seat their customers at the bar rather than at tables. When I inquired about it, I learned that the percentage of single people in Japan is rising each year, as fewer Japanese marry. The reason, I was told, is that over the past few decades, Japanese women have entered the workforce, gained financial independence, and started valuing their freedom. If they were to marry, they would not only lose that freedom but also be expected to care for their own family as well as their husband's, often at the expense of their own identity.

As I sat at the bar, I introduced myself to the people next to me. On my left was a highly paid young British engineer visiting from Korea, who travels there every six weeks from the UK and occasionally stops in Tokyo for rest and recreation. On my right was an older retired Australian couple from Brisbane. We had a delightful evening of food and conversation. Interestingly, when discussing the Peace Memorial Museum, the Aussie man remarked that the paradox of Hiroshima's bombing is that if the bomb hadn't been dropped, the war might not have ended. He added that the story of the attack boys only reinforced that point. I hated to admit it, but his argument had some foundation.

It struck me then how futile it is for humans to expect lasting peace in this world. Achieving peace would require human nature and emotions to evolve, yet there's little evidence to support that possibility. Over the past two millennia, humans have made enormous material progress, but our nature and vices—pride, greed, wrath, envy, lust, gluttony, and sloth—remain unchanged.

On Tuesday morning, just after 8:00 a.m., I walked to the ferry terminal on the opposite side of the Peace Memorial to catch the 9:00 a.m. ferry to Miyajima. I arrived early to purchase a return ticket. Upon disembarking on Miyajima Island, I was met by our local guide, Inati. We only had three hours on the island, so he got straight to business. The first thing Inati pointed out was the presence of deer everywhere—about 100 in the town and thousands more in the wooded mountains above. He then showed me the granite post marking the island's designation as a UNESCO World Heritage Site, which includes the Itsukushima Shinto Shrine and a small portion of the island. Interestingly, "Miyajima" means "shrine island," and "Itsukushima-jinja" means "worship island shrine." Only about 3,000 people live on the island, and only on the reclaimed land. There are no schools or hospitals; everything must come from the mainland. This reflects the Japanese respect for boundaries, acknowledging that the island shrine belongs to the supernatural, not to humans.

Later, as we stood on a curved beach at high tide, Inati pointed out the mountain in front of us, which is said to represent a reclining Buddha. We then passed through a granite gate guarded by two large creatures, part dog and part lion. One had its mouth open, and the other was closed, symbolizing the "ah" and "om" of breath and life.

We continued walking until we could see the vermillion-colored *o-Torii* (the Grand Gate), the largest in Japan. Historically, it welcomed pilgrims arriving by sea. This was the eighth *o-Torii*, last built in 1875, made of massive natural camphor trees with a circumference of 10 meters. Heavy stones weighing four tons were placed under the top beam, and the entire structure weighs 60 tons, which is why it stands firmly on the sea floor. Nearby, a plaque commemorates Helen

Keller, the blind American author and disability activist, who visited the island in 1937 and again in 1948, before and after World War II.

We walked through several open cloisters with vermilion pillars, passing the Marōdo Shrine, the main Itsukushima Shrine, the Daikoku Shrine, and the Tenjin Shrine, before exiting past the Takabutai and the elevated stage. Next, we visited the Daishoin Temple, home to 500 statues, each with a unique expression but all wearing red beanies. The temple has several attractions, including the Wisdom Sutra cylinders along a stone staircase. Turning each cylinder is said to bring blessings, and my fear of missing out compelled me to turn every single one. Legend has it that Yoko Ono showed one of these sutras to John Lennon, inspiring the song "Imagine."

A newer extension to the temple features a statue of the Buddha and a colorful sand mandala created during the Dalai Lama's visit in 2006, marking the shrine's 1,200th anniversary.

There were many other temples high in the mountains that I didn't have time to visit, nor did I explore the nature walks and climbing paths through the Misen Primeval Forest. But since I had nothing to prove, I wasn't bothered. I had seen what I needed to see.

I parted ways with Inati at 1:15 p.m., grabbed a sandwich and grapefruit juice for lunch, and boarded the ferry at 1:40 p.m. I was back at my hotel by 2:30 p.m. That afternoon, I meditated on the day's journey. In the past, I might have been judgmental about the worship of a thousand Buddha statues. Today, I have the mental space to accept what I don't fully understand, without judgment. God, the Source, the Universe—whatever you call the supernatural—cannot be compartmentalized. It exists outside time and space, and however humans define it is true, but it's only one facet of something infinitely greater.

That evening, I joined the Best of Hiroshima food tour, which I had arranged with Lukas and Barbara, my Swiss friends from the Osaka food tour. We had another wonderful evening exploring Hiroshima's food stalls and restaurants, accompanied by an Australian Irish couple. Later, Lukas and Barbara invited me for a drink at the rooftop bar of the Knot Hotel, where they were staying. We spent two enjoyable hours chatting over drinks, and by 11:00 p.m., I took my leave and walked two blocks back to my hotel.

On Wednesday morning, I woke up at 7:00 a.m., finished packing, and went up to the 25th floor for breakfast at 7:30 a.m. My taxi arrived at 8:45 a.m. to take me to Hiroshima Station for my 9:43 a.m. Shinkansen to Kyoto.

CHAPTER 18

Kyoto
15th – 18th May

At 11:20 a.m., I stepped onto the station platform in Kyoto (population: 1,459,640), Japan's seventh-largest city and former royal capital. I walked to the subway, added another ¥1,000 to my IC card, and boarded the Karasuma Line to Marutamachi Station, four stops away. I emerged at exit four, walked 100 yards, and there it was—my hotel, the Noku Kyoto, right in front of me. My room was amazingly spacious. In fact, I had two rooms: a bedroom and a lounge. Even the bathroom was split into three spacious areas: a washroom, a shower room, and a toilet.

I can't avoid mentioning the one thing that impresses or astonishes visitors to Japan: their toilets. Every single toilet in all the hotels and restaurants I've visited so far has been made by a brand called TOTO (it must be a billion-dollar company). TOTO not only manufactures the ceramic toilets but also the electronic panels with varying levels of sophistication. There are different flushes for big and small jobs, heated toilet seats, a button to spray water upward (like a bidet), and another button to dry the area. I've never been fond of bidets, so I'm embarrassed to admit I didn't try the wash-and-dry feature TOTO offers.

That afternoon, my guide for a four-hour tour of Kyoto was Akio Miyoshi, or Aki for short. He planned to take me to temples, the geisha neighborhood, and the backstreets of Kyoto. Frankly, I was already "templed out" from Miyajima, so my heart sank at the thought of visiting more temples. Nevertheless, I kept an open mind and didn't protest.

Aki hailed a taxi to take us to Sanjūsangendō Temple, where after passing through the temple gate, we removed our shoes and entered. The first thing that caught my eye was the 1,001 statues of the Buddhist deity Kannon—500 on one side, 500 on the other, and a giant seated statue in the center. The statues are made of Japanese cypress. At each end stood powerful, dynamic statues of the thunder god and the wind god, on raised pedestals. Between the 12th and 14th centuries, the Japanese worshipped these deities for good harvests. In front of the 1,001 statues were 28 additional statues, meant to protect the deity and the faithful. Aki explained that Buddhism originated in India, traveled through China, and eventually reached Japan.

At intervals throughout the temple, there were boxes for offerings, and visitors could purchase small plywood plaques to write their wishes. For a small donation, priests would authenticate certificates. The biblical story of Jesus and the moneylenders in the temple came to mind.

We left the temple and took a taxi to the Yasaka Pagoda. As we arrived, we saw mostly women—and a few men—parading in colorful floral kimonos. Aki pointed out that most of these were tourists from other Asian countries. We continued walking until we reached the Gion district, home to the geishas.

Sadly, I didn't see any. Apparently, they attend school during the day and return in the evening to dress elaborately for their dinner companions. Aki showed me the three streets in Gion where geishas live, their houses proudly displaying their names in large Japanese script.

We stopped for coffee—my treat—and Aki helped me locate two department stores, including Daimaru, where I could look for a kimono. Both attempts were unsuccessful. We then walked for 30 minutes back to the hotel, where we parted ways. Exhausted, I decided to skip dinner out. Instead, I stopped at FamilyMart, a convenience store next to my hotel, and bought a bottle of still water, a sandwich, and a banana. After eating in my room, I took a shower and called it a day. I had a long day ahead of me tomorrow.

On Thursday, after breakfast, I waited in the hotel lobby for my guide, Akira Ishida, who was to take me on the Discover Arashiyama tour. Akira was an elderly man, small in stature, wearing a plaid jacket, a straw trilby hat, and round brown plastic glasses. He looked like an English professor. He introduced himself and explained that the drive to Arashiyama would take about 25 minutes. As soon as we set off, it began to rain, but by the time we arrived, it had stopped.

Our first stop was Otagi Nenbutsu-ji Temple, perched on a mountainside with steep steps leading up to it. Above the temple was a dense forest. Originally built in 766 in Gion, Kyoto, by Emperor Sutoku, the temple was washed away by floods 50 years later. The current building dates to the 12th century, but the hall and gate were moved to their present location in 1922 for preservation. In 1955, Kocho Nishimura (1915–2003), a Buddhist monk, sculptor, and restorer, was appointed chief of Otagi. Over 10 years, starting in 1981, he restored the buildings and created 1,200 carved statues, known as *Rakan* ("the worthy"), the highest title for Zen Buddhist disciples. These statues, each with a unique face and expression, were carved by pilgrims under Nishimura's guidance. One statue is deliberately placed upside down, on purpose, as a maverick.

We left the temple and walked to Gio-ji Temple, also known as Ojoin Temple, whose main building was constructed in 1895. Inside is a statue of Taira no Kiyomori, a 12th-century chieftain, and four statues of nuns, one of whom is Gio, a great beauty who renounced the world after losing favor with her overlord, Kiyomori. It's a story reminiscent of medieval European folklore.

We continued walking until we reached a bamboo forest, a pure visual delight. A panoramic photo on my iPhone captured the bamboo trees curving at the top, forming a natural monastic archway. We passed through a lotus-covered lake and another bamboo forest before reaching Tenryū-ji Temple, a massive temple with imperial connections and UNESCO World Heritage status. Its Zen Garden, with a lake, rocks, flowers, and a forested mountain backdrop, was breathtaking. *Tenryū-ji* means "heavenly dragon." It was established in 1339 by the shogun Ashikaga Takauji (1305–58) as an act of penance for killing Emperor Go-Daigo in battle. The temple has been ravaged by fire eight times, most recently in 1864, but the gardens are today as they were when first built. As we left, we noticed five white horizontal lines on the yellow-painted wall, signifying its royal connection.

Akira hailed a taxi to take us to lunch at Musubi Cafe, where we both had chickpea curry with rice, a salad, bean soup, and tea. Afterward, we took a subway train to Kyoto Station, where Akira helped me board bus number four to Shijō Kawaramachi for some shopping. On Teramachi Street, I wandered into a secondhand kimono shop and finally found my kimono—actually, a *yukata*. As I handed it to the salesperson, I heard two women speaking English and recognized their voices. It was the two English women from Osaka, also trying on kimonos. What were the odds? We exchanged a few words before I left.

Many of these temples remind me of the churches scattered across the British Isles and much of continental Europe. Temples and shrines, cathedrals and churches, priests and faithful, prayers and money—the foundations of both were essential for the mental, emotional, and spiritual security of the working people. Notables, whether Japanese or European, donated money to build these temples and churches, ensuring their salvation in this life and the next. The five white lines indicating imperial approval on temples seemed no different from the royal coat of arms in British churches and chapels.

The coexistence of the temporal power of the emperor and the spiritual power of the temple priests is no different from what we see in European history. In Judaism, God is named Yahweh, a name formed from the initials used to address Him. In Christianity, we have a triune God—one God in three persons: the Father, the Son, and the Holy Spirit. In Islam, there is only one God, yet He is described with 99 adjectives. In Shinto, the original religion of Japan, God is nature itself; therefore, there are no names, no places of worship, and no scripture. In Buddhism, there are over a thousand gods—one for each human problem. I've reflected on these religions, each carrying strong cultural overtones. In my view, I don't see any contradiction between them, though the rational mind would invariably disagree. I see a paradox in which all realities point to one truth: all is in God, and God is in all. Everything else is simply our clumsy human effort to explain the inexplicable and to shape beliefs that fit within the narrow bounds of time and space.

Friday was a day of rest: no guided tours, but I had two places to visit—Nijōjō Castle and Kinkaku-ji Temple.

After breakfast, I made my way to Nijōjō Castle, a 15-minute walk from my hotel. As I approached, I noticed a wide moat running below the castle walls. I managed to get a ticket for entry, along with an English audio guide to help me navigate the grounds. Once through the main gates, I spotted a large watchtower at one corner of the castle. I was told there were originally four watchtowers, as one might expect, but two had burned down some time ago. Fires have destroyed many historic buildings in Japan, and most of what remains are recent reconstructions. I walked further in and passed through a large doorway into the inner courtyard. The ceiling above the entryway featured an elaborate artwork, predominantly gold, with several colorful panels.

Nijōjō Castle, a registered UNESCO World Heritage Site, has witnessed some of the most significant events in Japanese history over the 400 years since it was built. This should come as no surprise, given that Kyoto was once the royal capital. The castle was completed in 1603 on the orders of Tokugawa Ieyasu, the founder and first shogun, who unified Japan and ushered in a period of over 260 years of peace and prosperity.

I lined up to enter the Ninomaru Goten Palace, where we were instructed to remove our shoes and refrain from taking photographs. The palace consists of six connected buildings arranged diagonally from the southwest to the northwest. It has 33 rooms and over 800 tatami mats, with painted panels replicating the Kanō school's artistry. The castle served as the shogun's residence during visits to Kyoto to meet the emperor. The reception rooms featured tiger and hawk panels, designed to intimidate guests, while other rooms were adorned with cherry blossoms and flowers representing the four seasons, creating a welcoming atmosphere for counselors and visitors. One of shogun Hidetada's daughters, Princess Masako, became the consort of Emperor Go-Mizunoo in 1620. After the castle was repaired in 1619, Princess Masako set off from Nijōjō Castle in a grand procession with an enormous retinue to the imperial palace.

In 1867, the political rule of the Tokugawa shogunate came to an end, and power was restored to the emperor during the Meiji Restoration, which was proclaimed at this very castle. On October 13, 1867, the 15th shogun, Tokugawa Yoshinobu, summoned senior vassals from 40 domains to solicit their opinions. He then announced his intention to return power to the imperial court, though there was some resistance. In 1868, Edo Castle (now Tokyo Castle) was handed over without bloodshed, marking the beginning of a new era in Japanese history.

Before leaving the castle, I wandered through its beautiful gardens: the Zen-like Ninomaru Gardens, Plum Tree Grove, Cherry Tree Grove, Honmaru Garden, and Seiryū-en Garden.

I left at 10:15 a.m. to visit one of Japan's most famous temples: Kinkaku-ji Temple, also known as the Golden Temple due to its gold-painted roof. This Zen temple belongs to the Shōkoku-ji school of the Rinzai Buddhist denomination. Originally the Saionji family's villa, it was transformed in 1397 by Yoshimitsu, the third shogun of the Ashikaga shogunate, into the Kitayama Palace, centered around the golden stupa (Kinkaku). The temple became a center of politics and culture during Yoshimitsu's reign. After his death, it was converted into a temple according to his will. Since 1994, it has been a registered UNESCO World Heritage Site. The temple complex includes living quarters for the abbot and monks, teahouses, a belfry, a pavilion, and a hall.

On my way back, the taxi dropped me off at a food hall in Kyoto Kawaramachi, where I enjoyed a bowl of Japanese soba noodles with okra. As I walked back to my hotel, I noticed a stand selling fresh strawberries dipped in dark chocolate. I couldn't resist—they were absolutely delicious!

In the early afternoon, I treated myself to an 80-minute full-body massage at Kayco Vivid, Tripadvisor's top-rated massage parlor in Kyoto. My masseuse, Michiko, was exceptional—she played my body like a violin, leaving me feeling rejuvenated and relaxed.

On Saturday morning, I woke up late after nearly 10 hours of sleep, still feeling tired—likely due to the massage. By 8:00 a.m., I had checked out of the hotel and was on the subway. I added another ¥1,000 to my IC card and took the Karasuma Line from Marutamachi Station to Kyoto Station, just four stops in seven minutes.

CHAPTER 19

Mount Koya
18th – 20th May

I took an express train from Kyoto Station to Shin-Ōsaka, and it was so crowded that I had to stand with my heavy backpack for the 23-minute ride. At Shin-Ōsaka, I boarded the busy Midōsuji Line subway to Namba Station, a 50-minute journey. Upon arriving at Namba Station, with the help of the Google Translate app and a kind Japanese woman, I managed to find the Nankai Namba platform heading to Mount Kōya (or Koyasan, as it's called in Japan). An hour and a half later, at 12:45 p.m., the express train pulled into Gokurakubashi.

Koyasan is a sacred Buddhist site established by Kobo Daishi (Kukai) in the 9th century. With a population of 2,500, including 700 monks, it is a religious city like no other in Japan. At its heart are two major sacred sites: Danjo Garan, established by Kukai as a dojo for esoteric Buddhism, and Okunoin, the mausoleum enshrining the "Great Priest." There are 117 temples in Koyasan, 50 of which offer temple lodgings for pilgrims and visitors.

At Gokurakubashi, a station official directed us to a red cable car, Swiss-built, that carried about 30 people. In 15 minutes, we reached the top of the mountain in Koyasan, where several buses were waiting to depart. I was told that bus 22 would take me to my ryokan, the monastic hotel Ekoin, which means "Bless the Light." After nine bus stops, I disembarked at Ekoin and walked up to the reception. A monk named Gunnar, a German, greeted me and showed me around the monastery before leading me to my room.

My room reminded me of the film *The Last Samurai*, where Tom Cruise's character stays with the widow of the samurai he has killed. It featured sliding wood-and-paper doors, tatami mats, an oriental rug on the floor, a low black ebony table, and four cushions. Strangely, there was also a TV (which I never used), a safety deposit box, and a Japanese painting of a bird on a branch. The enclosed veranda had two proper chairs with legs and cushions, along with a coffee table at an appropriate height, where I could journal.

At 2:00 p.m., I ventured out to the main street and found a local food bar. I ordered soba noodles in a spicy onion soup and some vegetable tempura, a simple yet satisfying meal.

At 4:30 p.m., I headed to the meditation hall, where guests were invited to assemble for an Ajikan meditation. For 30 minutes, the monk, called Nano, guided us through two meditation techniques, starting with instructions on how to sit properly. It wasn't easy for someone like me, whose pelvis doesn't rotate as freely as those nimbler than I am. Nonetheless, I didn't judge myself. I've learned to accept and love myself, faults and shortcomings included.

Back in my room, a dutiful monk served my vegetarian dinner. Following the monk's suggestion, I started with the miso soup before moving on to the rest of the meal, which was served on a tray: rice, tempura, a vegetable hotpot, and an array of small dishes, including fermented foods and tofu in three different colors and shapes. I managed to eat everything, and while each dish tasted unique, I couldn't identify many of the ingredients. The monastery serves only shōjin ryōri, a vegetarian meal that excludes meat, fish, dairy, eggs, onions, and garlic.

At 6:45 p.m., I changed into white undergarments and a blue yukata and went to the onsen. I soaked in the hot spring water for 20 minutes, then took a shower. It felt like a deeply enjoyable ritual. When I returned to my room just after 7:00 p.m., the monks had already prepared my futon bed. I was ready to slowly unwind and reflect on the day.

On Sunday morning, I woke up at 6:00 a.m. and prepared for the morning service at 7:00 a.m. in the temple. The pitter-patter of rain on the stones outside my room was already audible. Thankfully, the journey to the temple was entirely indoors, through connecting corridors—much like in Benedictine monasteries in England. When I was ready, I made my way to the temple, joining others who were also heading there. I was one of the last to enter before the sliding doors were closed, and the service began with the monks' chanting. After 10 minutes of listening to the rhythmic Buddhist mantras, I found myself slipping into a hypnotic trance. While the sound of the Buddhist chants isn't as immediately captivating to me as the Gregorian chants of Benedictine monks, it was still effective in quieting my thoughts.

One of the monks then invited us to contribute by placing incense in the burner. He demonstrated how to do it: kneel in front of the burner, take a pinch of incense with your thumb and forefinger, bring it to your forehead, and then place it on the burner. Afterward, place your hands in prayer mode, bow, and move aside so the next person can follow. This process allowed everyone in the congregation to participate, ensuring the incense burned at a steady pace. When the service ended, we lined up to bow before the statue of Buddha before leaving. In the past, I might have hesitated at the idea of bowing to a foreign god, but now I go with the flow, embracing the experience without resistance.

Next, we were ushered into an outdoor area adjacent to the temple for a fire ritual called *soegomagi*. Participants could write a wish, along with their name, on a small piece of plywood measuring eight inches by two inches. For ¥500 (about $3), the plywood would be included in the ceremony. During the ritual, two monks chanted, one intermittently beat a drum, and another monk, dressed in a brown ceremonial cloak, sat in front of a small fire. Once everyone was seated, the monk in the brown cloak stoked the fire by throwing in various concoctions to intensify the flames. When the fire was roaring, he slowly placed the wish-laden plywood prayers on the grill, creating an enormous crackling blaze. After the ceremony concluded, we were ushered out, but not before bowing to three statues with baskets of fresh food placed in front of them. It seemed that the monks who eventually ate from these plates were considered blessed, as the food was an offering to the gods.

By 8:00 a.m., I was back in my room. My futon had been cleared away, and my breakfast table was already set up. The meal included a variety of vegetables, soup, tea, rice, and even two pieces of pineapple. Later, I asked the young monk who came to collect my tray, "What does *kikyo* (the name of my room) mean?" He told me it refers to a purple balloon flower.

I couldn't help but notice how hard the Buddhist monks work. They cook, serve, and clean up meals. They prepare futon beds in each room every evening and remove them in the morning. The toilets are cleaned every hour, on the hour.

It's nonstop work for these monks, who never seem to loiter or waste a moment.

Unfortunately, the relentless rain prevented me from hiking in Koyasan's beautiful mountain forests. Instead, I spent the day meditating and journaling.

Reflections on a Rainy Day
I use the journal prompts from the book *Choose You* by Helen Marie.

Q: What am I feeling right now?

A: My mind and spirit feel foggy and despondent, almost as if I'm experiencing helplessness and hopelessness. I feel lost and displaced. The rain outside isn't helping.

Q: Where am I feeling this emotion in my body? What sensation am I feeling?

A: I'm feeling it in my chest and heart. It's a sensation of sinking, as though something heavy is pressing down on me.

Q: When have I felt this emotion before? Reflect on past experiences. Is there a pattern?

A:

1. When I had to leave home for boarding school at the age of 10, which made me deeply sad. I hated having to leave home after each vacation.
2. When I've had to say goodbye to friends because life took us in different directions.
3. When I've made the difficult decision to let go of romantic relationships due to circumstances beyond my control.

Sometimes, when I am sad, a part of me wonders whether my 40 years of marriage were a waste of precious time. Of course, my rational mind knows they weren't wasted. For the most part, it was a good partnership, and we had the love and privilege of raising two wonderful, courageous, and intelligent daughters. I am deeply grateful for the joys of marriage and fatherhood. Yet now, I must accept and alchemize my feelings of sadness, which exist on several levels.

First, there is the sadness that my marriage came to an end. Even though the divorce was amicable, it was profoundly painful. Second, my daughters are now adults, pursuing their own lives. While I love them deeply and will always feel a sense of responsibility for them, I know I must learn to release this protective instinct, which is a difficult habit to break. Third, I spent 17 years funding a litigation to protect my wife's family assets. Despite winning many legal battles, the matter remains unresolved, and I've had to let it go. It saddens me that after all these years of struggle, I am neither victorious nor defeated—my goal remains unattained. Fourth, I miss my youthful energy and sometimes yearn for the financial stability of my past career. The person I once was is now gone, and I still mourn that loss. Who I am going to become remains a mystery. I am in this challenging, liminal state of "unknowing," where the present moment is all I truly have.

I admit and accept that I struggle emotionally with all types of loss in my life. I remind myself to be gentle and give myself time to grieve and mourn. I remember the good times and sometimes yearn for them, even though that time has passed and cannot return. Yet, I still feel love—almost a devotional love. Devotional love is something I've felt for as long as I can remember, though I wasn't fully aware of it until Raquel Spring, my fourth-generation astrologer, pointed out that my astrological chart confirms this tendency. Not everyone understands what devotional love is; some even consider it naïve. Yet, to me, it is the highest form of love.

Continuing my reflections:

Q: If I could name the emotion, what would it be?

A: Sadness.

Q: What are my thoughts about this emotion saying right now?

A:

1. My thoughts are saying that I'm sad because I don't like change when it comes to the emotional aspect of my life. Intellectually, I love change. I encourage and even promote it, but emotionally, I struggle with goodbyes. How can I pivot my emotional perspective on goodbyes?
2. My thoughts are about my loved ones. Earlier, I read a poem by Kukai, the monk and founder of Koyasan, which resonated deeply with me:

    "Although it is said that it is impossible to be disturbed by anything upon reaching enlightenment, I could not help but cry upon bidding farewell to a loved one."

This is exactly how I feel about the people I love.

Q: What is the emotion trying to tell me? What lessons, insights, or messages are there in the emotion?

A: The emotion is telling me that I still love all the people who have touched my life, even if our circumstances and relationships have changed. Nothing can alter the love between us, but

I must move forward with my heart and mind because going back is not an option. In fact, going back would not be an act of love but one of sentimentality. The lesson here is that it's okay to feel sad when we miss loved ones. We can send them love energetically, and they will receive it. The insight is to remember this the next time I feel sad.

Q: Is something deeper being triggered? How can I offer myself gentle compassion here?

A: Yes, something deeper is being triggered. Whenever I feel sad, I must recognize that it's the love within me seeking expression. So, in the future, when I'm sad, I'll send love energetically to my loved ones and engage in activities that bring me joy. A deeper trigger here is that sadness is pointing me toward love and joy in my life—moving from scarcity to abundance. Just as I eat when I'm hungry, I must seek joy when I'm sad. That said, the paradox is that there is a time for weeping and a time for laughter (Ecclesiastes 3:4). Perhaps the insight is to understand that weeping and sadness are also okay, so I must avoid being judgmental.

Q: What action is the emotion trying to tell me to take?

A: First, to allow this emotion, like a rainy day, to take its course, but then to act and move forward.

Q: How can I look at this emotion from a different perspective? In what way can I reframe the thoughts underpinning the emotion?

A: Sadness can be a beautiful and even seductive emotion at times. As Rumi says, a love that is not physically present can feel easier to love, and we can romanticize it. I can reframe the thoughts underpinning this emotion by viewing sadness as rain. We may not like it, but it's necessary to water the seeds of joy. If we didn't weep, we wouldn't know the joy of laughter. The next time I encounter a day of sadness, I'll think of it as a rainy day. This, too, shall pass, so I'll spend time on myself and my inner journey.

Q: What tools can I use to bring my body back to a sense of safety?

A: I'll use breathing techniques: first, breathing in through one nostril and exhaling through the other, and vice versa; second, taking a deep breath in through the nose and exhaling with a long "ah."

Q: Who can I reach out to for support?

A: My ex-wife, my daughters, my brothers, and my friends.

Q: What steps can I take to soothe myself? What self-care practices are in my kit?

A: Embracing myself with my arms and saying, "George, you are deeply, deeply loved."

I'd like to close this reflection with a quote from Rumi:

> *"Awaken dear soul, the truth awaits beyond the veils of illusion and despair. Sadness and sickness, mere phantoms, dissolve like morning mist in the sun's embrace. So laugh, my friend, laugh heartily, for life's paradoxes and fleeting woes are but a shadow cast upon the screen. Remember the truth. You are the dreamer and the dream. The laughter and the tears. The seeker and the sought."*

* * *

At 12:30 p.m., I went out for lunch at Hanabashi, a restaurant on the main street. I ordered a vegetarian bento box with hot saké—a pure delight. To work it off, I considered visiting Danjo Garan, a grand temple complex with a pagoda and main hall, but I felt I'd overdone temples for now. Instead, I chose the Reihokan Museum, which houses about eight percent of all certified national treasures in Japan. Afterward, I returned to my ryokan to enjoy green tea and a sweet in my room. Dinner would follow, and then a hot spring bath and shower before retiring for the night.

On Monday morning, I was up at 6:00 a.m. and ready for the morning service at 7:00 a.m. The first time experiencing something is always magical; the second time, not so much. I also attended the fire ritual again, this time placing a plywood stick with the following words:

> *"Untie the knots in my heart, my mind, and my life. Remove the 'have nots,' 'may nots,' and 'might nots' that find a home in my heart. Release me from the 'could nots,' 'would nots,' and 'should nots' that obstruct my heart, my mind, and my life. And most of all, remove from my life all the 'am nots,' especially the ones that whisper to me that I am not good enough."*

After the ritual, I returned to my room for breakfast—a traditional Japanese meal. As I ate, I noticed and observed my feelings. I found myself missing my English breakfasts. How interesting it is that we yearn for things from the past, which can pull us away from what is yet to come. I'm aware of this tendency, and for now, that awareness is enough. I don't judge myself; I simply observe. It's already 8:30 a.m., and I must be out of my room by 10:00 a.m. to catch the cable car from Koyasan back to Osaka, the Venice of the East.

CHAPTER 20

Osaka
20th – 22nd May

I took an earlier train from Gokurakubashi and arrived at Hotel Zentis in Osaka around 12:30 p.m. I checked in immediately, retrieved my suitcase—which they had stored for a week—and went up to my room on the eighth floor. After changing into fresh clothes, I took my dirty laundry to the second-floor coin laundry, loaded it into the washing machine, and headed to the hotel restaurant. There, I ordered a light sandwich, fries with wasabi mayo, and an iced peach tea.

After lunch, I returned to the laundry room to transfer the clothes to the dryer and came back 45 minutes later to collect them. My suitcase was now ready to be sent to my hotel in Tokyo, saving me the hassle of lugging it to Mount Fuji, my next destination. I showered, dressed, and headed to Teppanjinja Kitashinchi, a teppanyaki restaurant serving a wide variety of delicious skewered meats and seafood. After three days of a vegetarian diet, I was craving meat—no judgment. Dinner at Teppanjinja was glorious. I had nine skewers of meat, seafood, and vegetables, along with two glasses of red wine, which helped me sleep soundly that night.

On Tuesday, I woke up at 6:00 a.m. but stayed in bed for another 30 minutes. In the hotel restaurant, I ordered an American breakfast, but it was still distinctly Japanese: cold ham slices, salad, weak scrambled eggs, and yogurt. I asked for a boiled egg instead of scrambled eggs, and it took 15 minutes—likely because it became a special order. I refused to let it upset me and consoled myself with an extra glass of grapefruit juice. *Arigato gozaimasu*—I am very grateful. At breakfast, I decided to explore the Osaka Museum of History. I walked 15 minutes to the subway and took the Tanimachi Line (purple line) from Higashi-Umeda Station. I was surprised by how few locals seemed to know locations in their own city. After asking several people—with the help of Google Translate—I finally found the station, just five yards from the last person I'd asked. After three stops, I alighted at Tanimachi Yonchome Station and walked five minutes to the museum, only to find the entrance shut. A notice on the door stated that the museum is closed on Tuesdays. I took a deep breath and didn't allow myself to cuss.

Earlier, on my walk to the museum, I had noticed Osaka Castle nestled in a public garden much like Central Park, just a few minutes away. As I've said countless times, the Universe has my back. I walked 15 minutes through the park to the castle's wide moat, its water the color of aquamarine. The exterior walls of this castle dwarfed even the large stones of Kanazawa Castle. As I walked through the gates, I realized, looking at the map, that there was not only an outer moat and wall but also an inner one. It was an extraordinary castle. The iron gates of the inner portal were almost nine inches thick. The castle itself was a combination of a fortress and a pagoda, with two sets of elevators and stairs—one for going up and one for going down.

I was directed to the fifth floor, where I was immersed in scenes from the 1615 Summer War in Osaka. These were vividly displayed on a folding screen and a model battlefield layout encased in glass, showing how troops from both sides were positioned moments before the battle began. I was in my element: I've always had a young boy's fascination with warfare, yet paradoxically, I harbor an intense dislike for the pain and suffering wars inflict on humanity.

Since the fifth floor also incorporated the sixth floor, I explored both before heading up to the seventh floor, which celebrated the life of Hideyoshi Toyotomi (1537–1598). Hideyoshi built Osaka Castle and succeeded in unifying Japan. Born into a poor farming family, he rose from humble beginnings to become the nation's ruler. However, history reveals that Hideyoshi was not universally loved. His rigid collection of land taxes and his aggressive invasion of the Korean Peninsula, which included taking hostages, caused widespread suffering. He also sent messengers to the Philippines, Taiwan, and Okinawa, demanding their subjugation. Hideyoshi adopted many sons but was 57 when his biological son, Hideyori, was born.

In a brutal turn, Hideyoshi executed his adopted son, Hidetsugu, along with more than 30 others—including Hidetsugu's wife, mistresses, and children—on the pretext of rebellion. Hideyoshi died in 1598 at 62, but not before asking his advisers, including Ieyasu Tokugawa, to support his son Hideyori after his death. However, events led Ieyasu Tokugawa to be appointed shogun in 1603, establishing his shogunate. He attacked Osaka Castle in 1614 and 1615, forcing Hideyoshi's concubine, Yodo-dono, and his son Hideyori to commit suicide, effectively eliminating the Hideyoshi Toyotomi clan.

Reflecting on this story, I concluded that karma is truly a bitch, and no one can escape it. Hideyoshi rose from poverty to power but was consumed by it, ultimately destroying his own family to secure his son's future. In doing so, he severed all potential support for Hideyori, making it easy for Tokugawa to seize power. While Hideyoshi built an incredible castle, Ieyasu Tokugawa expanded and fortified it even further.

Given that Ieyasu Tokugawa managed to seize Osaka Castle, it makes sense that he would want to fortify it further. To give you an idea of the castle's size, the total length of its walls is 12 kilometers. The number of stones used for the walls is estimated to be between half a million and one million. The highest section of the wall is about 90 meters tall. The granite stones were gathered from several different regions, including the Rokko and Ikoma mountains. The production and transport of such a massive volume of stone required a huge labor force and considerable technical skill. Stones were moved coast to coast, loaded onto ships, unloaded, and transported by land to the construction sites. While all of this is undeniably impressive and surely created employment for many, I can't help but wonder—is this mankind's destiny? Must we labor and suffer? Are we, as a species, condemned to endless cycles of toil and slavery, age after age, era after era? An interesting detail is that Osaka Castle is twinned with Sforza Castle in Milan, whose ruling family, the Visconti, had an equally brutal history.

I left the castle and stopped at a nearby coffee shop for a mango yogurt drink, which was delicious in the 26-degree heat. Following Google Maps, I made my way out of the castle grounds to Tanimachi Yonchome Station. From there, I took the Tanimachi Line (purple line) to Tanimachi 9-chome Station, changed to the Sennichimae Line (rose line), and rode to Namba. After a 10-minute walk, I arrived at Dotonbori, greeted by an explosion of neon lights and entertainment. Even in daylight, I was mesmerized by the endless arcade of shops, food stalls, and vibrant energy.

I chose to dine at Ganko Sushi, a fine dining establishment founded in 1963. My meal included three large tempura prawns, a bowl of soba noodles in a hot pot with chives, and a plate of sushi featuring 10 pieces of different fish. While I recognized salmon, tuna, and prawn, the others were unfamiliar but equally delicious. I washed it all down with half a pint of Asahi beer, leaving me a happy camper—all for ¥4,620 (about $29). Incredible value. On my way back to the hotel, I couldn't resist three candied strawberries on a stick. As I bit into them, the flavors exploded on my taste buds, transporting me to heaven.

Back at the hotel, I finished packing and took my suitcase downstairs to the reception for forwarding to my final stop, Hotel Gracery Asakusa in Tokyo. In the evening, I took a 10-minute taxi ride to Yakitori Zen, where I enjoyed a two-hour meal of skewered meats and vegetables presented in small, delightful bites. The chef grilled everything just two meters away from me, serving only chicken and duck, with occasional grilled vegetables. To ensure no one left hungry, the final dish was purple rice with a curry soup poured over it. I started with an Asahi beer and followed it with a glass of New Zealand Pinot Noir. The meal concluded with a cup of mint tea and two small, flambéed squares of the Japanese version of crème brûlée. What a gastronomic delight!

On Wednesday, I woke up at 6:20 a.m. and went down for breakfast at 7:00 a.m. As I was getting my grapefruit juice, I encountered an Australian couple who didn't have Australian accents. The man dropped a stirrer and bent down to pick it up. It looked precarious, so I said, "Mind your back." They both chuckled, and he replied, "So, you know my history." I responded, "I don't know yours, but I know mine."

After breakfast, as I headed toward the elevator, I saw the same Australian couple again and struck up a conversation. They invited me to join them, so I sat down—I still had an hour to spare—and we had a wonderful chat. Merrilyn, in her sixties, is the daughter of English parents who moved to Australia. Her mother never allowed her to lose her English accent or adopt an Australian one, which explained my initial confusion. Her act of rebellion was marrying a man with a Cockney accent. Keith, her husband, in his seventies, emigrated to Australia from London. Raised in Islington, he considers himself a Cockney because, back then, he could hear the Bow Bells from that distance. The official definition of a Cockney is someone born within the sound of the Bow Bells, the bells of the Church of Saint Mary-le-Bow, founded in 1080.

Keith—or "Keef," as he'd say in his Cockney accent—doesn't have a strong accent naturally, but he can put on a good show when he wants to. He's a former chartered accountant, and Merrilyn was a ballet teacher. A few years ago, they decided to go on a gap year. They sold their house in Sydney, bought a caravan trailer and a four-wheel drive, and traveled across Australia before settling in Perth, Western Australia—much to the shock and horror of their children. Now, they're touring Japan, seeking new adventures. They've also volunteered for four months in Tanzania, helping an Australian woman maintain a school for thousands of Tanzanian children, aiming to shape the country's future. What an incredible project—imaginative, visionary, and mission-driven. I loved hearing about it.

Reluctantly, I parted ways with them and made my way to the taxi that would take me to Shin-Ōsaka Station.

CHAPTER 21

Mount Fuji
22nd – 24th May

My journey from Shin-Osaka to Mishima via Nagoya on the Shinkansen took two hours. From Mishima, I boarded a Fuji Kyuko bus to Kawaguchiko, the town near Mount Fuji, arriving just after 1:30 p.m. after a 90-minute ride. Although the city of Fuji has a population of 245,015, nearly one million people live within 30 kilometers of Mount Fuji.

Upon arriving at the Mount Fuji View Hotel, I encountered my first hotel booking mishap of the trip. The front desk couldn't locate my reservation. We tried everything, but nothing worked. Reaching out to my travel agent in the UK was pointless, as it was too early for them to respond. I then searched online for the contact number of their Japanese agents in Tokyo but couldn't find it. Thankfully, I located it on the paper version of my Japan itinerary. A woman named Claire answered—her English accent was a comforting sound. I asked if she spoke Japanese, and she said yes, so I handed the phone back to the front desk staff. They spoke in Japanese, and the woman at the desk made very positive noises on my end. I was asked to wait while a room was prepared, so I used the time to write in my journal. After an hour, the woman at the front desk approached me with a warm smile and introduced herself as Yoko. I couldn't resist asking, "As in Yoko Ono?" She laughed and said yes.

As Yoko escorted me to my room, she told me that John Lennon and Yoko Ono had visited the hotel in 1978. Unfortunately, they didn't see Mount Fuji because it was hidden behind clouds. Lennon had drawn a sketch of the mountain with a question mark where the peak should be, and that sketch is proudly displayed in the lobby. Today, Mount Fuji was equally shy, veiled behind clouds. I hoped I'd get a glimpse of her tomorrow.

Dressed in my green yukata and feeling like a VIP, I headed to the onsen for a hot spring bath before my early dinner at 5:45 p.m. Just as I was about to enter, I noticed a sign: "No tattoos allowed." I'd been warned about this in London, but this was the first time I'd encountered the restriction. I called Yoko, who asked me to come upstairs. She gave me four patches to cover my tattoos, and I was able to enjoy the hot springs for about 25 minutes. Afterward, I showered, shaved, and returned to my room—only to find, to my shock, that Mount Fuji had unveiled itself in all its glory.

I grabbed my iPhone and started shooting videos and photos—panoramic and close-up—of this magical mountain. It always happens when you least expect it. I love magic and mystery; we need it in our lives. I captured the moment because I didn't know if the mountain would reappear in the next day or two. At 5:45 p.m., I went down for dinner and was seated at a corner table overlooking the greenery behind the hotel. I had chosen French cuisine for the evening, and the meal—featuring fish and red meat—did not disappoint. Neither did the unnamed Japanese red wine.

Reflections on Self-Love

I use journal prompts from the book *Choose You* by Helen Marie:

Q: What are some self-limiting beliefs that you would like to work on?

A: Off the top of my head, there are two:

1. I have a self-limiting belief that in this selfish and self-absorbed world, I will not find the devotional love I am seeking.
2. I have a self-limiting belief that I will not succeed financially without immense effort and without compromising my integrity.

Q: What areas of your life would you like to make changes to?

A: First, I want to make changes to my living situation—perhaps maintaining a small base in London while renting overseas or even relocating to another country. I'm not sure yet. Second, I want to change my work environment by finding a suitable partnership with a larger organization. This would allow me to focus on what I love most: research, writing, and teaching.

Q: What are three compliments you could give yourself?

A: I'm highly creative, I have charisma, and I'm an excellent communicator.

Q: What are the things, and who are the people that energize you?

A: The things that energize me are learning, teaching, speaking, writing, and filming. The people who energize me are intelligent, empathetic, sensitive, humble, and loving.

Q: What are the things, and who are the people that drain you?

A: The things that drain me are managing accounts, running a business, and feeling pressured. The people who drain me are arrogant, demanding, and unempathetic.

Q: What boundaries do you feel you need to put in place?

A:

1. Being authentic and meaning what I say, even if it's unwelcome.
2. Saying "no" more often so I can say "yes" to myself.

Q: What's something in your life that you would like to let go of?

A: The drudgery of endlessly creating content for social media. I want someone else to handle that for me.

Q: What is something you would like to forgive yourself for?

A: I would like to forgive myself for my role in the breakup of my marriage. I would also like to forgive myself for failing to conclude my litigation matter, which I feel let down my ex-wife, my daughters, and my parents.

Q: What would help you feel more content?

A: Feeling confident in myself and my work, experiencing self-love and love from others, and slowing down my pace to fully enjoy what I co-create.

Q: How can you give yourself a break?

A: By doing what I can each day as best I can—without rushing, guilt, or blame.

Q: What is the one thing you can do today for your mind, body, and soul?

A: To enjoy my life without haste and to be fully present in the moment.

Q: What things are you grateful for?

A: I'm grateful for everything in my life: my family, my ex-wife, my daughters, my loved ones, my work, my books, my health, and my life itself.

Q: How can you love yourself a little more?

A: By being kind, gentle, loving, and compassionate toward myself.

* * *

On Thursday, I woke up early at 5:45 a.m. and couldn't resist opening the windows to sneak another peek at Mount Fuji. Most of the mountain was visible, but a shroud of clouds was fast approaching. After washing and dressing, I checked again and saw the peak, though much of it was now obscured.

Mount Fuji (12,390 feet) holds a significance for the Japanese much like what Mount Ararat (16,854 feet) means to the Armenians. Mountains hold physical, spiritual, and cultural importance for humans. They are the world's water towers, providing between 60 and 80 percent of all freshwater resources. Without water, there is no life. Water is life, and thus it is deeply linked to spirituality, as it nurtures and nourishes people not only physically but also spiritually and culturally. For example, for Armenians, Mount Ararat is a spiritual, cultural, and national symbol. For the Greeks, Mount Olympus represents their history and culture. For the Jews, Mount Zion is where God made a covenant with King David, and the word "Zion" is used not only for Jerusalem but also for all of Israel.

Today, I planned to explore Lake Kawaguchi, one of the five lakes surrounding Mount Fuji. I wanted to enjoy a 20-kilometer walk and see the mountain from different perspectives. I'd take the local red bus to the farthest stop, Akebono, and then walk back, stopping for sightseeing along the way. If I got tired, I could always hop back on the bus to shorten the route.

After breakfast, I took the 8:30 a.m. hotel shuttle bus to Kawaguchiko Station, where I boarded the red line bus that circumnavigates Lake Kawaguchiko. I paid ¥1,500 (about $10) for an all-day pass and rode the bus to stop number 20, Oishi Park, home to the Kawaguchiko Natural Living Center.

The Kawaguchiko Natural Living Center is a beautiful garden by the lakeshore, with vibrant purple flowers arranged to frame Mount Fuji in the background. I took several photos and enjoyed a soft-serve ice cream with vanilla and blueberry swirls. I walked back to bus stop 20 and waved down the bus just as it was about to leave. My next stop was bus stop 15, the Music Forest Museum. After paying the entrance fee, I found myself in what could have been mistaken for a Swiss village, with floral arrangements designed for photos of Mount Fuji. This wasn't really my scene, so I walked back to the bus stop and hopped on the next bus to stop number 9, the panoramic ropeway—a cable car offering a unique perspective of Mount Fuji.

I waited in line for 30 minutes, chatting with a young British couple to pass the time. Soon, we were at the top platform, greeted by a spectacular view of Mount Fuji and the world below. Twenty minutes later, I was back in line to descend. By the time I reached the bottom, I was famished and searched for a restaurant. I ordered soba noodles with tempura and an extra-large bottle of Asahi beer.

By 2:00 p.m., I was back at the hotel and took an hour-long nap. When I woke up, I journaled for a while, then dressed in my yukata and headed to the onsen for the last time. This time, I had the chance to sit in an open-air onsen. The cold air touching my head and shoulders created a beautiful contrast to the heat enveloping the rest of my body. Before heading downstairs for dinner, I came across a question that intrigued me, and I wanted to delve deeper.

"To better understand yourself, George, find out why you want what you want. Getting to the emotions you're after. To go even deeper, ask yourself why you think you can't feel those now."

Q: What do I want?

A: I want to feel fully alive, with love and joy in my work and personal life.

Q: Why do I want what I want?

A: I want to feel fully alive, with love and joy in my life, because life is short. I want to make each day count as a lifetime, knowing all we truly have is the present moment.

Q: Why do I not feel that now?

A: I do feel it now, but only in short bursts. I want these bursts to last much longer.

Now that these questions have been asked, they cannot be unasked. I want to wake up each day feeling blessed to do the work I love. I'm writing a new book—the one you're reading.

I'll engage in interviews with other professionals in the space, continue teaching The DARE Method®, and still have time for creative thinking. I want to wake up each day knowing I belong to a tribe and am forging new friendships. I want to live in this space.

Friday morning, I woke up at 5:00, likely because I'd slept at 8:30 p.m. I washed, dressed, journaled, had breakfast at 7:30 a.m., and headed to Kawaguchiko Station. My 9:59 express train to Otsuki took about an hour, and the ride from Otsuki to Shinjuku, Tokyo, took an hour and 20 minutes. From there, I took two subway lines to reach Asakusa.

CHAPTER 22

Tokyo
24th – 25th May

I arrived at my hotel, Gracery Asakusa, at 1:30 p.m., checked in, and collected my suitcase, which had arrived from Osaka. I showered, laundered my smalls, socks, and t-shirts, then went out for an ice-cold caramel latte and a baby chocolate croissant, which staved off my hunger for a few hours. Returning to the hotel, I took out my laundry and packed it. After resting a bit, I headed out for an early dinner at 6:00 p.m.

Google helped me find a yakitori restaurant just a five-minute walk from my hotel. The restaurant, Torihei, caught my attention with a photograph of grilled chicken on a skewer. That, along with a small jug of saké, was all I needed. Three people worked behind the counter: an older woman—possibly the mother-in-law—and a younger woman, both involved in cooking; and a man who took my order and seemed to be managing the accounts. I imagined he might be the younger woman's husband. Just as I finished my meal, two young Japanese women walked in and sat next to me.

They were attractive, well-dressed city girls. I wrote a few kind words of thanks in English on my Google Translate app and showed the Japanese translation to the man. He erupted in joy and called out to the women in the kitchen. The young woman on my right grabbed my phone, asking, "What did you write?" I showed her, and she said, "That's so nice of you." We ended up chatting. I ordered another small jug of saké, and the conversation turned to US politics after she mentioned she had lived in St. Louis, Missouri.

After breakfast on Saturday morning—my last in Japan—I checked out of my hotel room, left my luggage with the concierge, and made my way to the Tokyo National Museum, which opened at 9:30 a.m. I spent several hours exploring just one of its six buildings: the Japanese Gallery, housed in a stunning Art Deco structure with a sweeping central staircase. For three hours, I wandered through four distinct sections across two floors, covering the arrival of Buddhism, Buddhist art, the culture of the Imperial Court, Zen ink painting, tea ceremonies, and the arms and armor of the Samurai. From the 12th to the 19th century, the exhibits included paintings on folding screens and sliding doors, sculpture, lacquerware, ceramics, swords, and much more. Naturally, I was drawn to the arms and armor of the Samurai, along with the history of Japanese swords, the master swordsmiths, and the science behind forging blades for the warrior class and the decorative artwork on the sheaths. By 12:30 p.m., I had finished my visit to the Tokyo National Museum and was on my way back to the hotel in Asakusa.

By 1:30 p.m., I arrived at Shinagawa to catch my 2:24 p.m. train to Narita International Airport for my flight to Vancouver. At the airport, I checked in my bag, cleared customs, and searched for something to eat. I found an entire floor dedicated to Japanese cuisine and opted for my usual: udon noodles with lobster, shrimp, and vegetable tempura. With 30 minutes until boarding, I headed to the gate for my Japan Airlines flight, JA18.

66 days completed.

14 days remaining.

PART 5

CANADA

"When I am in Canada, I feel this is what the world should be like."

Jane Fonda
Actress

Canada

CHAPTER 23

Vancouver, British Columbia
25th – 27th May

My Japan Airlines flight provided me with an experience I'd never had before: reliving the same day twice. I had already enjoyed my last Saturday in Tokyo, and now I was about to experience the same Saturday all over again in Vancouver. How is this possible? By crossing the International Date Line (IDL). Crossing the IDL eastbound means losing a day, while crossing it westbound, as I did, means gaining a day.

My flight arrived in Vancouver around midday on Saturday. I took an Uber to the Loden Hotel, a boutique hotel in the downtown Coal Harbour area. After checking in and settling into my room, I came down for lunch at Le Tableau, the on-site French bistro. I spent the rest of the day relaxing in my room, meditating, and journaling. This was a luxury I rarely allowed myself in the past, as I was always on the move, always doing something. Now, I was luxuriating in the time I had given myself to be present and generous to myself. The universe had gifted me an extra day, and I didn't squander it—I spent it entirely on myself.

On Sunday, I woke up at 6:00 a.m. and was downstairs for breakfast at Le Tableau by 7:00 a.m. I indulged in a proper Canadian breakfast: two fried eggs on sourdough bread, five slices of crispy bacon, a sophisticated mini hash brown cake, and two cups of Americano. By 8:25 a.m., I was out walking in the rain to Cycle City Tours and Bike Rentals for a three-hour cycling tour of Stanley Park. When I arrived at 8:45 a.m., the six other cyclists were already there, trying on helmets, adjusting bikes, and donning ponchos. I discovered that Vancouver (population: 2.65 million) is a very wet city, with more rain than London, earning it the moniker "Raincouver" or "Rain City." Nevertheless, with the help of our guide, Brian Spanier, we set off single file across busy streets in the direction of Stanley Park.

Stanley Park is like no other city park. Covering a thousand acres (over 1.5 square miles), it was established in 1888 and occupies the northwestern tip of the downtown peninsula. It's larger than New York's Central Park and half the size of London's Richmond Park, though Richmond Park isn't technically in central London. Named after British Governor General Lord Stanley, who granted it to the Vancouver City Council for $1 per year, the park boasts over half a million trees, some towering as high as 76 meters and hundreds of years old. We cycled around Coal Harbour, past Beaver Lake, through a rainforest, and emerged at the Lost Lagoon. The rain didn't let up. My poncho covered the handlebars, protecting my hands and most of my body, but every time I returned to my bicycle seat, it was wet. As a result, the seat of my jeans and the lower half of my trouser legs were soaked. Strangely, I was enjoying the experience. With a beginner's mindset, I embraced it as joyfully as my inner child would have jumping in a puddle just for the fun of it.

We stopped at Prospect Point Cafe for a hot drink and a much-needed break for our bums. Outside the café, there were First Nations totem poles—some modern and multicolored, others original carvings on tree trunks. Originally, totem poles told the stories and histories of the tribes, though many eventually rotted away. Our final stop was in the rainforest, where Brian pointed out the oldest Douglas fir, over 800 years old, and one of the oldest majestic cedar trees. Brian then led us back toward Coal Harbour and downtown, returning to the cycle shop.

I returned to my hotel famished and ordered a hamburger, fries, and a ginger beer. After resting in my room for half an hour, I headed to the waterfront at 3:10 p.m. to find the Harbour Air Terminal. Once I located it, I went to the ticket reception area to get my ticket for the journey once known as the "mail run" to Salt Spring Island, specifically to Ganges Village, the island's capital. Salt Spring Island is one of many islands in the Strait of Georgia, between Vancouver Island and the mainland of British Columbia.

The de Havilland Otter Turbine DHC-3T, with its design reminiscent of Charles Lindbergh's *Spirit of St. Louis*, is a beauty to watch as it takes off and lands. Its wings sit above the fuselage, and its single engine and propeller-driven floats allow for remarkably short take-offs and landings. It was pure joy for me. The flight took 30 minutes each way. I spent about 90 minutes roaming Ganges Village, which caters mainly to its 10,000 residents and half a million annual tourists. In that time, I covered every street in the village and revisited every shop up to three times. While waiting at the landing, I met a long-time local resident picking up a friend from London. We exchanged a few words, and she shared that many new residents on the island don't engage with the local community—they remain secretive, hiding behind their walls. Hearing this sad reality on such a beautiful island left me with a sense that I'm on the right path in my life: exploring, connecting, and growing.

On Monday, my alarm woke me at 7:00 a.m. after a poor night's sleep. I had woken at 1:00 a.m. and again at 3:00 a.m., unable to fall back asleep until 4:00 a.m. I showered, dressed, and was downstairs for breakfast by 8:15 a.m., where I met Tammy Vigue, a retirement coach based in British Columbia. Though she lives four hours northeast of Vancouver, she was in the city for family reasons. We had a long chat over breakfast that lasted just over two hours. We agreed to continue these conversations and even shared a wish to host a retreat together, perhaps in Sedona, Arizona. After Tammy left, I checked out of my hotel, left my luggage with the front desk, and spent three hours walking around downtown. I returned to the hotel just after 1:30 p.m., collected my luggage, and ordered an Uber to take me to the railway station.

CHAPTER 24

VIA Rail: The Canadian
27th – 28th May

I arrived at Vancouver's Pacific Central Station, a magnificent stand-alone building. After checking in, receiving my ticket, and handing over my luggage, I prepared to board the train. The Canadian, as it's called, travels from Vancouver to Toronto, and I would disembark at the eighth stop: Jasper, Alberta, my destination. By 2:30 p.m., I was on board train number 2, car number 11, seat number 3—a cabin measuring 130 by 90 centimeters. To put it in perspective, it was smaller than Nelson Mandela's jail cell.

Sitting in my cabin, I studied the route guide from Vancouver to Toronto. There were seven stops before Jasper. From Jasper to Edmonton, two stops; from Edmonton to Saskatoon, Saskatchewan, five stops; from Saskatoon to Winnipeg, Manitoba, five stops; and from Winnipeg to Toronto, Ontario, 10 stops. The total distance is 2,740 miles, with a minimum duration of four days, depending on delays caused by rail cargo traffic.

The cabin steward, Thierry, a young, light-haired Canadian man with a ponytail and black-painted nails, showed us how the toilet worked, how the bed folded down over the toilet, and the location of the single shower in our car—which resembled a horizontal coffin. Thierry seemed cold and unfriendly, and I wondered if he was in the wrong line of work. Still, his demeanor was none of my business, so I didn't take it personally. I reminded myself to stay in the role of an observer.

I chose the 5:00 p.m. dinner slot in the restaurant car, as the only other option was 8:15 p.m., which felt too late for me. Dinner felt reminiscent of the Orient Express: white linen tablecloths, silverware, and glassware. The only thing missing was Hercule Poirot. I started with squash soup, served with a bread roll and butter, followed by a rack of lamb with mashed potatoes and pak choi, all washed down with a glass of Merlot. My dining companions were French Canadians from Quebec, returning home. Our conversation centered on the differences between France and Quebec, and Canada and Quebec.

* * *

Reflections on Coming Home to Yourself
I use the journal prompts from the book *Choose You* by Helen Marie.

Q: What does 'coming home' to yourself mean to you?

A: Coming home to myself means I don't have to act, please others, or behave in ways that seek acceptance or validation. It means being authentic. My heart, mind, and spirit are in harmony. I say what I mean and mean what I say. I'm also striving to stay humble, though it's not an easy task.

Q: How does it feel?

A: It feels liberating and comforting.

Q: What three words would you choose?

A: Authentic, sincere, and humble.

Q: What are the things that make you feel most you?

A: Speaking my mind and heart without fear or favor, though sometimes silence is prudent. Moving away from negative people and energy. Being enthusiastic about my work and the people I'm with. Good humor, wit, and laughter. Feeling empathy for the suffering of others.

Q: Describe that feeling.

A: I feel enthusiastic, cheerful, and energetic.

Q: Where do you feel it in your body?

A: In my chest and belly.

Q: How can you create space to do more of them?

A: By moving away from energy that drains me and toward people and communities that energize me.

Q: Who are the people that make you feel most you and why?

A: People who are ready to grow, learn, and enrich their lives through teaching, meditating, and evolving.

Q: What are the things that don't align in your life and that drain you?

A: Reluctantly aligning with others' expectations for commercial or political reasons and conforming to social or political correctness. These no longer align with me and drain my energy.

Q: What are the ways you could set boundaries around these?

A: By listening to others, respecting their opinions, and stating my own views without offending. If that doesn't work, I withdraw from the connection.

Q: What are the things that are stopping you from being who you want to be?

A: My limiting beliefs.

Q: How can you remove these barriers?

A: By believing in myself, trusting that I am deeply loved, and deserving of joy, happiness, success, and all forms of wealth.

Q: How can you cultivate a healthier relationship with yourself in terms of meeting your needs, the way you view yourself, and incorporating more self-compassion and kindness?

A: By accepting myself as a fragile, flawed human being who is neither perfect nor strong. I need love and intimacy. I must be more compassionate and kinder to myself, viewing myself with less judgment and more observation. My need for money doesn't make me greedy, nor does my need for sex make me a pervert.

Q: How can I open space to be more deeply honest with myself and listen to my inner wisdom?

A: By being honest about the relationships I want to cultivate in the next chapter of my life. If I can't devote myself to one person, perhaps I can devote myself to a cause. In work, I should explore different business partnerships.

Q: What is your inner wisdom saying? How can you create time to listen inward more?

A: My inner wisdom struggles with the competition between different parts of me. I want to cooperate with the different parts of me, so that the sum is larger than the parts. I want the warrior, the nurturer, and the achiever within me to cooperate, making my life bloom. I'm failing forward toward that goal.

Q: How do I create time to listen inward more?

A: Through morning and evening meditation, and by sauntering in nature each day, as nature has much to teach us.

Q: What three words could you use to describe your inner, core self?

A: Authenticity, sincerity, and humility.

Q: What is a promise to yourself you could make today to connect a little deeper to yourself going forward?

A: I promise to show up as my beautiful, authentic self in the present moment.

* * *

On Tuesday morning, I woke up at 5:30 a.m. in my cell-like cabin. Sleep had been a struggle, not just because the bed was unusual, but because I had to get up twice—once at 1:00 a.m. and again around 3:00 a.m.—to empty my bladder. Each time, I had to lift the bed and push it back into the wall to access the toilet seat beneath it. Adding to the challenge, Canadian cargo trains passed by throughout the night. I was reliably informed that in Canada, cargo trains take precedence over passenger trains. First, because the cargo train companies own the tracks, and second, because cargo is the big moneymaker. These trains have powerful lights and blare their horns as they pass, a process that can take a long time since they often consist of more than 200 container-length cars and stretch up to five miles long. They require three locomotive engines—one at the front, one in the middle, and one at the back—to pull them at a slow, steady speed. Just when you think one train has passed, another begins. Canada needs to be fed from one end to the other, importing, exporting, and distributing goods. The truth is, Canada, like Australia, isn't just a country—it's a continent.

I got dressed, packed my backpack, and headed to the dining car, where breakfast was served from 6:30 a.m. While enjoying a marvelous meal of eggs, bacon, and toasted sourdough bread, we were informed that due to cargo traffic delays the previous night, we had made little progress. Instead of arriving in Jasper at 11:00 a.m., we would likely arrive around 3:30 p.m. What we weren't told was that our clocks would move forward an hour as we entered mountain time. As a gesture of goodwill, the head waiter offered us a sumptuous lunch of vegetable soup, chicken pot pie, and vanilla ice cream. The train finally pulled into Jasper around 5:00 p.m.

I disembarked, took several deep breaths of fresh mountain air, and collected my luggage from under a canopy near the station exit. I then set out to find a taxi to my hotel, the Marmot Lodge. Outside, a group of four Englishmen were also waiting for a taxi to the same hotel. Luckily, I hitched a ride with them; Jasper taxis only accepted cash, and I had none. After checking in at the Marmot Lodge, I had dinner next door at Evil Dave's Grill, where I enjoyed a dish called El Diablo, a flavorful chicken and beans plate. Soon after, I showered and went to bed, utterly exhausted.

CHAPTER 25

Jasper, Alberta
28th – 31st May

On Wednesday, I woke up at 5:30 a.m. and got out of bed half an hour later. After washing and dressing, I went to the front desk. Since the hotel didn't offer breakfast, they directed me to the Forest Park Hotel next door, where a buffet breakfast cost C$20, all included. I enjoyed my usual breakfast there and then walked to Jasper's Main Street, about 20 minutes away. I arrived at the information center at 8:30 a.m., but it didn't open until 9:00 a.m., so I explored the town, browsing shops, eateries, and points of interest.

My travel agent had strongly recommended the Jasper Skytram, a gondola established in 1964 that takes visitors to Whistlers Summit (not to be confused with Whistler Mountain in British Columbia). The panoramic views from the gondola were breathtaking. Jasper (population: 4,600) is surrounded by towering, snow-capped alpine mountains, arguably more majestic than the Swiss Alps or New Zealand's Southern Alps. From the summit, you could see the town nestled in a sea of forests and lakes.

The enormity of the Rocky Mountains dwarfed everything—the Athabasca and Miette rivers, Beauvert, Annette, and Edith lakes, and the Valley of the Five Lakes further south. The mountains had names, making them feel personable, though many were hard to remember. I wrote them down to keep track: Mount Colin, Roche Bonhomme, Grisette Mountain, Mount Dromore, Mount Tekarra, Amber Mountain, Antler Mountain, Mount Hardisty, Mount Kerkeslin, Signal Mountain, and many others. The highest, Mount Robson, stood just under 13,000 feet. Being so high among these majestic peaks, I couldn't help but feel awe at the immensity and power of nature—and how insignificant we are as humans. This was enough awe for one day. I had nothing to prove to myself or anyone else. I wanted to absorb this feeling and wallow in the joy and beauty I'd experienced.

I returned to the Summit Cafe for a cup of Earl Grey tea, followed by a wonderful bowl of bison chili con carne with garlic bread for lunch. I noticed how my body relished the hot food in the cold climate.

On the way up, the gondola was crammed with 20 people, but on the way down, I was the sole passenger, accompanied by an Australian operator who clearly loved his job. I returned to the Jasper Adventure Centre, where Katie, a young lady who had helped me purchase my Skytram ticket and arrange the shuttle, assisted me in planning a hiking itinerary for the next day. It included biking around the three lakes: Beauvert, Annette, and Edith. She strongly advised renting bear spray for C$10 from a nearby pharmacy, as I'd be hiking in bear, elk, and moose territory during cub-rearing season, making any perceived threats potentially fatal.

I then decided to get a haircut to tidy up my buzz cut, which had grown out unevenly since Melbourne six weeks earlier. A haircut always leaves me feeling renewed. As I wrapped up my journaling for the day, I headed to a café for a light salad dinner.

On Thursday, I woke up at 6:45 a.m. After breakfast at the Forest Park Hotel, I met up with the 40-odd people on the Colette tour, who were preparing to head to Lake Louise. I'd previously met some of them on the train from Vancouver to Jasper. Later, I returned to my room for a 70-minute Zoom call with a CNBC editor interested in my views on retirement and pensions from the perspective of young people.

I then walked to a pharmacy to rent bear spray, as advised, and proceeded to see Katie at the Jasper Adventure Centre to hire an electric bicycle for my tour of the lakes. Wearing my hard helmet—which had the word "NUTCASE" etched in capitals on the front, much to the amusement of my family and friends who saw my photo—I placed my personal effects in the front basket and my hiking stick on the back panel. I set off just before 11:00 a.m.

It took 10 minutes for me to realize I didn't know where I was going. At the train junction, where cargo trains rolled in constantly, I asked several people in their cars if I was on the right road. They all apologized for not being locals. I continued until I reached a highway Katie had mentioned I'd need to cross. As soon as I did, I saw the signpost for Lake Beauvert, and my spirits began to rise. I cycled for another 15 minutes and soon arrived at a picture-perfect lake; its emerald-green waters so vivid they looked Photoshopped. I was already on the grounds of the Fairmont Jasper Park Lodge and golf course, a prestigious lakeside hotel that felt like a Disneyland for adults. I cycled to the main building and asked the bellboy where to park my bike. After parking, I went into the coffee bar and ordered a black Americano to kickstart my journey. By 11:45 a.m., I was back on my bike, heading for the northernmost lake, Lake Edith. Since modern homes lined its shores, I was compelled to cycle on the roads around it for about four miles, which I did.

Leaving Lake Edith, I took a wrong turn and lost some time, but I refused to let it bother me. I ended up cycling onto a highway, which was stressful due to fast-moving cars. I stopped where I could, consulted Google Maps, and found my way back to Lake Edith. From there, I cycled down to Lake Annette, which was much more enjoyable thanks to a beautiful walking path encircling it. Cycling was forbidden here, so I locked my bike to a metal post and walked the lake's perimeter, about three miles long. The walk was delightful, with the lake's aquamarine and turquoise waters glistening under the sun. By the time I finished and returned to my bike, it was already 2:30 p.m.

Back on my bike, I continued to soak in the beauty of the lakes and mountains. There's a unique joy in feeling the wind blow against your face, especially when speeding up on an electric bike. The mountains looked even more alluring juxtaposed against the lakes and forests. It was breathtaking and spiritually uplifting. My eyes couldn't get enough of the scenery, and I couldn't help thinking this must be what heaven is like. I cycled back to the Fairmont Hotel for lunch: a hamburger, sweet potato fries, and ginger ale.

I returned my bike to the shop just after 4:00 p.m. Truth be told, I was knackered. I walked back to the hotel, stopping first to return the unused bear spray. I hadn't seen any bears, moose, or elk—perhaps tomorrow.

On Friday morning, I woke up at 7:00 a.m. and had breakfast in town for a change. Then, I returned to my hotel to rest until my 11:00 a.m. check-out. I spent two hours walking around town because the Brewster bus to Lake Louise wasn't due until 1:20 p.m. At 1:15 p.m., I boarded the bus, driven by a woman named Rose. The journey was scheduled to last three and a half hours with no stops. I was so captivated by the mountain views that, despite there being a toilet at the back of the bus, I didn't need to use it.

The 230-kilometer route, known as the Icefields Parkway or Route 93, is one of the most beautiful highways I've ever traveled. We passed Athabasca Falls and Sunwapta Falls. Shortly after, we noticed cars stopped on the road—clearly, something interesting was happening. As we passed, we saw mountain goats: two adults and a kid. Mountain goats resemble common goats but are related to antelopes and gazelles. They inhabit high-altitude regions to avoid predators.

At Parker Ridge Trailhead, we glimpsed the Saskatchewan Glacier and Mount Castleguard. Again, we saw cars stopped, this time for a large black bear grazing. I'd tried in vain to spot one during my bike ride the day before, but here it was. We passed the Glacier Skywalk but didn't stop to experience the glass-floored observation platform. Rose made a brief stop, allowing me to take some extraordinary photos.

The Icefields Parkway is the drive of a lifetime. According to *National Geographic*, it's one of the most spectacular driving tours in the world—I couldn't agree more. We also passed the Columbia Icefield Centre, the Athabasca Glacier, and the Saskatchewan River, a raging torrent winding through the mountains. As we passed Peyto Lake and Peyto Glacier, hidden behind a wall of Douglas firs, I knew we were nearing my destination. The first stop was my hotel, the Lake Louise Inn. Though the journey took three and a half hours, it felt like 10 minutes in my mind. That's what happens when you're having fun.

Cycling around the three lakes in Jasper National Park, Alberta.

CHAPTER 26

Lake Louise, Alberta
31ˢᵗ May – 2ⁿᵈ June

Lake Louise Inn boasts a scenic location at the base of several mountains in Banff National Park. While it's not a five-star lodging, it has almost everything you could want—except a view of Lake Louise itself. It features two restaurants, one formal and one informal. For dinner, I chose the informal option and had a Timberwolf pizza. I managed to finish it by removing the crust, effectively reducing it to a nine-inch pizza. I took my two-piece North Face jacket and fleece to the laundry and studied local maps for walks and hikes around Lake Louise. The town itself has a population of fewer than 700 people.

On Saturday morning, I woke up at 7:00 a.m. with a sore throat and a cold. I'd slept in a sweater, as I'd felt chilly overnight. In my dreams, the endless miles of majestic Canadian Rockies played on the screen of my mind—hundreds of mountains with names no one remembers.

After breakfast, I went to the concierge to adjust my plans for the day. The previous evening, I'd considered going whitewater rafting on the Kicking Horse River in the afternoon. But with a sore throat and a cold, I wasn't up for the challenge and decided to skip it. Instead, I opted to visit Lake Louise, the emerald-green (and occasionally aquamarine) lake. I left the hotel around 9:00 a.m. and took local bus number 11 to the Chateau Lake Louise, another Fairmont hotel. My plan was to walk around the lake, which is about two miles long (but tricky in places), and hike up to the Fairview Lookout for a higher perspective of the lake.

I attempted the Fairview Lookout first and was joined by an American couple staying at the Fairmont. We made it two-thirds of the way up before the icy ground became too treacherous. Along with a few others, I decided to turn back without judgment. It wasn't a total loss—we managed to capture some stunning photos on the way down.

At 12:45 p.m., I headed to the Chateau for afternoon tea. While pleasant, the sandwiches and cakes weren't as fresh as they should have been. It reminded me why afternoon teas in London are unparalleled—the devil is in the details. I returned to my hotel mid-afternoon to rest and wind down. The next day, I had an early start to catch the 6:20 a.m. coach to Calgary Airport.

On Sunday morning, I woke up at 5:00 a.m., well-rested. I was downstairs by 6:00 a.m., ready for my 6:20 a.m. pickup by Brewster Tours. The driver informed me that plans had changed. Since I was the only passenger on the large luxury coach, the new plan was to go to Banff, Brewster's headquarters, to catch an 8:00 a.m. coach to Calgary. This saved time, as Banff is an hour closer to Calgary Airport. It also gave me a chance to grab a bagel with cream cheese and an Earl Grey tea—coffee doesn't sit well with me when I have a cold. We left Banff at 8:00 a.m. and arrived at Calgary Airport by 10:00 a.m. My Air Canada flight to Quebec City via Montreal wasn't until 2:30 p.m., so I had plenty of time to read and journal.

Reflections on Feeling Calmer

I use the journal prompts from the book *Choose You* by Helen Marie.

Q: What are the three things you're grateful for?

A: My life, the people I love, and my purpose.

Q: What sensations do you notice in your body when you practice this gratitude?

A: I notice joy, love, calm, high energy, enthusiasm, a warm heart, relaxed muscles, and peace of mind.

Q: What self-care activities make you feel most at ease?

A: Journaling, walking in nature, being in and around water, and dancing.

Q: What are the things that bring you joy?

A: Being with my loved ones, connecting deeply with others, living near nature, writing, communicating, and dancing.

Q: How can you create more space?

A: By living near my daughters; finding a new home near nature and water; joining a new community to teach, learn, and debate; continuing to write; and creating a music playlist for dancing.

Q: What are the things that bring you the least joy?

A: Difficult and narrow-minded people, those uninterested in growing, individuals with low energy, and repetitive tasks like bookkeeping.

Q: What are the ways you can reduce these?

A: Avoiding difficult, low-energy people and those who don't resonate with me.

Q: What is bringing you the most worry today?

A: My expenses are higher than my income.

Q: What is the one small thing you can do to help alleviate that worry?

A: Manifesting opportunities for organizations to hire me to work with their clients and employees.

Q: What are some ways that you can be more present in your day?

A: Meditating, walking in nature, scheduling work slots for each activity, setting aside time for chair exercises (7 minutes), dancing (15 minutes), and cooking my meals.

Q: What self-care tools can you use to help feel calmer and a little more at ease?

A: Breathing exercises (candle breath, deep belly soul breath, alternate nostril breath), therapeutic body shaking, dancing, soothing self-touch, walking in nature, meditation, journaling, and practicing gratitude.

Q: What is your favorite way to relax?

A: Watching films and documentaries, swimming when possible, and walking in nature daily or whenever I can.

Q: What is one small thing you could add to each day to bring a moment of calmness for you?

A: Dancing for 15 minutes.

CHAPTER 27

Quebec City, Quebec
2nd – 6th June

I landed at Quebec City airport around 11:00 p.m. on Sunday night, and by the time I put my head on the pillow at Hotel Manoir Victoria, it was past midnight.

The next morning, Monday, I woke up at 9:00 a.m. Not once during this 80-day trip had I slept in so late, but I was exhausted after 20 hours of travel the day before. I dressed, had breakfast at the hotel, and was out the door by 10:30 a.m.

Quebec City, with a population of 733,516, spans over 1.5 million square feet, making it the eighth-largest city in Canada. It's also home to the largest fort in North America, perched 400 feet above the St. Lawrence River at the city's highest point. The city's star-shaped design, with four bastions, ensures 360-degree protection for the fortress and its surroundings.

I walked to the Musée de la Civilisation, only to find it closed on Mondays. Undeterred, I continued my walk and stumbled upon one of the activities I'd hoped to do in Quebec City: a boat tour on the Saint Lawrence River. The boat, named AML Louis Jolliet, offered a two-hour ride with historical commentary for $57. I eagerly paid and boarded.

The tour provided a view of Quebec from the water, accompanied by tales of battles between the French, British, and Americans. I've always loved history and stories. Louis Jolliet, the French Canadian explorer, is known for his discoveries in North America. In 1673, Jolliet and Jacques Marquette, a Jesuit priest and missionary, became the first non-natives to explore and map the upper Mississippi River.

One story that stood out was the storming of the cliff at what is now Wolfe's Cove, west of Quebec. On the night of September 12, 1759, the British Army, led by General James Wolfe, fought the French under the Marquis de Montcalm at the Battle of the Plains of Abraham. The British emerged victorious, but both commanders died from their injuries. Historians speculate that if Wolfe had lived, his devoted mentee, George Washington, might not have fought in the Revolutionary War 16 years later.

From the boat, we admired Montmorency Falls, which, though not as large as Niagara Falls, is 30 meters higher. We also saw Île d'Orléans (population: 6,817), an island in the Saint Lawrence River where inhabitants trace their roots to Brittany and Normandy in the 1600s. I found it interesting that our Samurai friend in Kanazawa, Masa, also traced his ancestry back to 1603, to the Tokugawa shogunate. In many places, modernity arrives at a glacial pace.

On the return journey, we spotted three red icebreaker ships, essential for breaking ice in winter when the Saint Lawrence freezes over. Once, people could walk across the frozen river, but in recent years, the ice has become too thin. We also saw the citadel and the Château Frontenac, now a hotel with over 600 rooms.

After disembarking, I wandered through Old Quebec until I came across an Italian restaurant called Va Bene. The name sounded appealing, and the outdoor seating under an awning looked inviting. I ordered ravioli with mortadella and pistachios, which was delicious, paired with a non-alcoholic Peroni beer. I wanted the taste of lager on a scorching 24-degree day (Jasper, according to my weather app, was still at 12 degrees).

A short walk later, I found a shop called Chocolato, where I had the most delicious ice cream: a small cone of soft vanilla ice cream entirely dunked in orange-flavored dark chocolate. My senses surrendered.

After lunch, I wandered toward the Château Frontenac, passing the old post office building, and soon arrived at the Basilica of Notre-Dame de Québec. The basilica is an impressive piece of architecture. Behind it, in the gardens above the staircases, stands a large statue of its founder, Saint Francis de Laval (1623–1708), known among Catholics as the Apostle to America. Laval left behind a life of privilege and fortune in France to build a New France in Quebec. When he arrived, there was nothing here. Over his lifetime, he founded parishes, churches, schools, seminaries, and mills, many of which still exist today. Approximately 100 entities bear his name: streets, lakes, mountains, parishes, hospitals, and even the third-largest city in the province of Quebec.

Written on a glass panel in the basilica, words attributed to Laval touched me deeply. I needed to hear this message today:

> *"Believe firmly that we must simply retain our faith in him and leave him to do his work."*

In short, it means, "Let go, let God." For years, I've prayed and believed this, but recently, I've felt I was running out of time, money, and faith. Laval's message recharged my hope to carry on and not give up.

I had an early dinner at the bistro Chez Boulay, enjoying a vegetable risotto and a crème brûlée—a delight to the senses. Afterward, I returned to my room for an early night.

On Tuesday morning, I woke up at 4:00 a.m. For some reason, I felt compelled to learn more about why America and Britain went to war in 1812, especially since Britain was already entangled in a war with Napoleonic France. I spent an hour scrolling through articles on my iPhone before succumbing to sleep again.

I woke up at 8:00 a.m. and left my room an hour later to visit the tourist information office at 12 Rue Sainte Anne. My curiosity about the War of 1812 lingered. I knew from history that the British had invaded Washington, D.C. and set fire to the White House and Congress. What I hadn't connected before was that, in the same year, the Americans had invaded Canada to expel the British from North America. Today, I discovered that the British not only defended Canada but also received support from the Québecois. The French Canadians believed their language and customs were already protected under British rule, whereas they feared American rule would lead to "Americanization." This story captivated me.

I arrived early at the tourist information office to purchase a C$75 ticket for a five-hour countryside tour the next day. The tour, departing at 10:30 a.m., would take me 35 kilometers northeast of Quebec City, along the Saint Lawrence River, through rolling agricultural land and the foothills of the Laurentian Mountains. The itinerary included Montmorency Falls, Île d'Orléans, and Sainte-Anne-de-Beaupré.

After purchasing my ticket, I went to find a bite to eat before my two-hour guided tour of Quebec City, and found Maison Smith, a charming patisserie and coffee shop that only the French could perfect. The queue was long but moved quickly as I chatted with an American family ahead of me. I ordered a Croissant Smith—filled with ham and cheese—and a cappuccino. Each heavenly bite and sip were pure enjoyment.

I returned to Rue Sainte-Anne, where we were supposed to meet our guide for the day, Paul Burrows. Paul was a short, slim man with a nearly full head of silver-white hair. He spoke French like a native Québécois but could switch to flawless English effortlessly.

Our first stop was the statue of Samuel de Champlain, a French explorer who made at least 20 trips to North America and founded Quebec City on July 3, 1608. Interestingly, no one knows what Champlain looked like, so the face on the statue is that of someone else. On the surface, this might seem like a trivial detail, but it raises questions about the accuracy of historical representations everywhere.

Next, we visited a house with red tiles, doors, and windows, now a restaurant called Aux Anciens Canadiens. This building once housed a family of 10, living without water or electricity and relying on an outhouse. It's the only surviving structure typical of that era, offering a glimpse into the harsh living conditions of the past.

Paul shared stories of the various battles fought by the French, British, and Americans to seize Quebec due to its strategic military value. The city's high vantage point offers a commanding view of the ocean and the rivers flowing into the Saint Lawrence from the Great Lakes and the Canadian border. The French successfully repelled two British attempts to invade but lost the third in 1759. General Wolfe, leading the British fleet, used stealth to attack Quebec City from the rear. His troops scaled the steep cliffs and hoisted cannons onto the Plains of Abraham, named after a local farmer. The French never expected an attack from this direction, believing it impossible. The British won the battle, but both Wolfe and Montcalm, the French commander, died. Wolfe fell during the battle, while Montcalm succumbed to his injuries two days later.

For centuries, Montcalm was buried in the church of the Ursuline convent. Recently, his remains were exhumed and reburied in a mausoleum alongside his soldiers. The Ursuline convent compound is vast and now serves as a day center, a preparatory school, and will soon provide accommodation for individuals deemed appropriate by the government.

Paul explained that much of the Catholicism once practiced fervently by Quebec's French-speaking population has faded. Many locals no longer identify as strong believers, and the Catholic Church's influence has significantly weakened. We then visited the Basilica Cathedral of Our Lady of Quebec, which I had seen the previous day. Adjacent to the basilica is a former Jesuit seminary founded by Bishop Laval. Today, the seminary operates as a co-educational school for students aged 13 to 18. Paul noted that all schools in Quebec City are co-ed due to the declining number of children. He also remarked that everything we had seen so far was within the walled upper city, where the grey stone architecture resembles that of Edinburgh, Scotland.

Leaving the upper walled city, we descended to the lower, historically poorer parts of Quebec, located outside the walls. Here, the streets narrowed but became more vibrant, lined with shops, restaurants, patisseries, chocolate shops, and cafés. The atmosphere reminded me of the backstreets of Nice, France, with its charming, bustling energy.

Around 12:15 p.m., our group parted ways with Paul. I made my way to the 1640 Bistro near Rue Sainte-Anne, where I ordered a Caesar salad with grilled chicken and a pint of non-alcoholic Heineken. While waiting for my food, I purchased an online ticket for $22 for an hour-long tour of the famous Citadel of Quebec.

After lunch, I headed to the citadel. Our guide, a civilian, provided background on the Royal 22nd Regiment, known locally as the "Vingt-Deux" or "Van Dooz." The regiment, headquartered in Quebec with 800 soldiers, has served in numerous conflicts and is currently training Ukrainian troops in the UK and Estonia.

We walked to the original gunpowder building, now a museum showcasing Quebec's military history. The exhibits included battle plans from Generals Montcalm and Wolfe, weapons like guns and swords used in the conflict, cannonballs of various sizes, and detailed model replicas of the battlefield.

We then walked to another section of the citadel, where we were shown the holding places for snipers. These positions are scattered throughout the citadel, strategically placed to provide a 360-degree view of the surrounding area. The aerial layout for the snipers forms a Star of David, ensuring that no attacker could succeed without being spotted. This design reminded me, in some ways, of Japanese castles, which also feature strategically built walls to repel invaders, though the methods differ.

Next, we were shown three significant buildings: the officer's mess, the commander's residence, and the Governor General's residence (the second official residence for the latter). The former hospital now serves as the regiment's headquarters, while the old jail has been converted into a museum dedicated to the history of the Royal 22nd Regiment.

We were then taken to the ramparts, where the cannons are positioned. This spot offered, without a doubt, the best view of Quebec City. I took as many photos and videos as I could, capturing the breathtaking panorama. On our way out, we passed the busts of three "Van Dooz" soldiers who had been awarded the Victoria Cross for gallantry beyond the call of duty. We also saw the Cross of Vimy Ridge, commemorating the Canadian soldiers who lost their lives in 1917 during the Battle of Vimy Ridge in France.

Dinner that evening was at Chez Rioux & Pettigrew, a restaurant recommended by my brother Chris, who is a self-proclaimed foodie. While I generally prefer simple meals, I occasionally enjoy indulging in a feast for the senses. The menu was written in poetic French culinary language, so I surrendered to the barman's expertise. He crafted a delightful aperitif to whet my appetite and recommended the special of the day, *Les Inspirationistes*, a four-course meal paired with French white and red wines. Each course featured a creative combination of meats, vegetables, and sauces, with portions small enough to leave me feeling satisfied but not overly full. The meal was both inspiring and a true work of art.

On Wednesday morning, I woke up at 7:30 a.m. and made my way to the hotel breakfast. I needed a solid meal to fuel me for the five-hour countryside tour. After breakfast, I stopped at Maison Smith to pick up a sandwich for lunch and enjoy one of their excellent cappuccinos.

By 10:20 a.m., I boarded the white Unitours coach, which was already nearly full. Our first stop was Montmorency Falls, where we were advised to take the gondola to the top and return to the coach within 60 minutes. I purchased a round-trip ticket for $17, joined the queue, and ascended in the gondola. At the top, we were greeted by a beautiful colonial-style building with a verdigris roof and verandas on both the ground and first floors. A circular garden adorned the front, featuring lush greenery, purple flowers, and a central water fountain. A sign above the entrance read "Manoir Montmorency," named after the same noble family as Bishop Laval. I discovered it was yet another restaurant.

I walked to the right of the building, heading toward the waterfall and the viewing platform above it. For some reason, I felt nervous as I approached, but I didn't resist the feeling. Instead, I took deep breaths, as my therapist advises, and moved forward. I took photos and a short video of the stunning view before making my way back to the gondola.

Soon after, we continued our journey to Île d'Orléans, an island in the middle of the Saint Lawrence River. The river is named after Saint Lawrence, as explorer Jacques Cartier discovered it on the saint's feast day (August 10, 1535). The island, approximately 20 miles long and 5 miles wide, lies three miles east of Quebec City and is home to about 7,000 residents spread across six villages. The island is primarily agricultural, with strict development restrictions that make it feel as though time has stood still.

We visited a few vineyards and apple orchards before stopping at the Chocolaterie. There, I purchased three orange slices dipped in dark chocolate as my dessert. Earlier, I had enjoyed a mozzarella, tomato, and pesto sandwich from Maison Smith, which I had brought along for lunch.

Back on the bus, we drove to an artisanal copper shop founded by the late Albert Gill. Today, the shop is managed by his second wife, two daughters, and a granddaughter. Over the years, many cathedrals and churches have commissioned works from Gill, including in our next stop, the town of Sainte-Anne-de-Beaupré (population: 3,063).

The Basilica of Sainte-Anne-de-Beaupré is surrounded by beautiful fields, as its name suggests (*Beaupré* means "beautiful meadow" in French). The cathedral is enormous—perhaps three times the size of the Basilica Cathedral of Our Lady of

Quebec—and its grandeur feels almost out of place in such a small town. This is especially striking given that less than 10 percent of Catholic Québecois now attend mass. The basilica's numerous chapels, intricate craftsmanship, and stunning artwork are magnificent, undoubtedly costing a fortune to create and maintain.

Near the cathedral stands a circular building that resembles a Shia Mosque. This structure, called the Cyclorama of Jerusalem, houses a massive panoramic painting that wraps around the interior walls, depicting scenes from the crucifixion of Jesus in Jerusalem. The painting was completed in 1882 by the renowned German painter Bruno Piglhein and a team of international artists, taking four years to finish. The artwork is divided into three conjoining panels: the first shows the city of Jerusalem, the second depicts the countryside to the west of the city, and the third portrays Calvary, the site of the crucifixion.

It was almost 3:00 p.m. when we returned to Quebec City. During the journey, I struck up a conversation with a lovely couple from Connecticut, Loretta and Bernie Andrews, who were sitting behind me. Loretta shared her dream of becoming a writer, and I hope our chat inspired her to take the leap and pursue her passion.

Reflecting on the Basilica of Sainte-Anne-de-Beaupré, I couldn't help but wonder how often we overreach in our pursuit of excellence, only to find that the most important element—love—is missing. I don't say this to criticize anyone, including myself; it was simply an observation. The artistry and craftsmanship at the basilica were extraordinary, on par with what you'd expect at Notre-Dame in Paris. Yet, it felt surreal to see such a grand structure in the middle of rural Canada. It made me question whether I, too, sometimes try too hard in my relationships and work. Perhaps if I focused less on perfection and more on love, my life would be more joyful, and the results more fruitful.

That evening, my last in Quebec City, I returned to Chez Boulay for dinner. I started with sautéed mushrooms, followed by a bouillabaisse dish, and finished with a maple mousse. The meal was delightful, paired with a glass of Quebec Malbec—a wine that rhymes and resonates in a way that feels uniquely Canadian.

As I dined, I felt a sense of clarity and connection to my higher self. I realized it was time to move on. As a father, I've gone above and beyond my duty, and even my daughters acknowledge this. Yet, an old mental habit holds me back: a lingering sense of guilt that by following my north star, I'm abandoning them. How insidious this feeling is! I know I must focus on myself first before I can truly help others. Even in my filial duty, I've done all I can for my ailing, bedridden mother, who now suffers from full-onset dementia. I must let go and let God, doing so with love and gentleness.

On Thursday, I woke up at 5:30 a.m. without an alarm. After washing and dressing, I packed my last-minute items and headed to the front desk to settle my bill. I left my luggage with the concierge and walked to Maison Smith near my hotel for their legendary Croissant Smith and a cappuccino. By 7:10 a.m., I was on my way to the Quebec City railway station, just two blocks away.

The train departed at 8:06 a.m., heading toward Montreal with at least six stops along the way. I arrived in Montreal (population: 1.75 million) at 11:30 a.m., three hours later. Rolling my luggage behind me, I made my way to the Avis car rental office, a few blocks from the station. The pedestrian walkways in Montreal were in such poor condition that they made New York City's sidewalks seem pristine by comparison. Even the

Avis office looked tired and in need of renovation, reminding me of Newark, New Jersey, in the mid-1980s.

I settled into a black Chrysler 300S sedan and plugged my destination—Montreal to Magog—into Google Maps. The trip was estimated to take two and a half hours. I was hungry and needed to use the restroom, but I decided to wait until I was out of the city. I set off at 12:30 p.m. and drove for an hour before spotting a Tim Hortons, a Canadian coffee shop chain. I stopped, used the restroom, and ordered a small rectangular pepperoni pizza and an iced peach tea. Feeling refreshed, I continued my two-hour drive to Magog.

CHAPTER 28

Lake Memphremagog, Quebec
6th – 9th June

I entered the town of Magog (population: 28,312) around 4:00 p.m. and arrived at my Airbnb, Dans Les Bras de Memphré, 10 minutes later. The owners, Ghislaine and Michel, warmly welcomed me and showed me around their home, including my room with an ensuite bathroom and access to a living room. Ghislaine handed me a list of a dozen local restaurants where I could enjoy a 10 percent discount. After settling into my room, Ghislaine kindly offered to take care of my laundry. I spent some time journaling, freshened up, and rested before heading out for dinner in town.

    I drove about 17 kilometers to the monastery, L'Abbaye de Saint-Benoît-du-Lac, hoping to attend Compline, the evening prayer chanted by Benedictine monks to usher in the night. However, I arrived early and found myself joining a prayer service at 7:00 p.m., with Compline scheduled to follow shortly after. Feeling exhausted, I decided to skip Compline and instead headed to Saint Michel, a restaurant on Magog's main street. There, I enjoyed breaded scampi on a salad, spaghetti

Alfredo, and a Heineken Zero. By 9:00 p.m., I was back in my room, lights out.

On Friday, I woke up at 6:30 a.m., washed, dressed, and as agreed, brought the rest of my laundry to Ghislaine. She preferred to operate her own washing machine and dryer. For breakfast, she had prepared a yogurt and berry parfait served in a martini glass, orange juice, and a croissant with egg, bacon, sausage, tomato, and lettuce. Her husband, Michel, served the meal along with a cup containing two shots of espresso and hot water to top it off.

Just after 9:00 a.m., I left for the abbey. When I arrived, I understood why a 2018 *National Geographic* photograph had featured the abbey as one of the most beautiful panoramic landscapes in Quebec. The monastery sits on the shores of Lake Memphrémagog, a freshwater glacial lake spanning both Newport, Vermont, in the United States, and Magog, Quebec, in Canada. While the lake stretches across both regions, most of it lies within Quebec, though most of its watershed is in Vermont.

I ventured downstairs to the monastery's boutique, where products made by the monks are sold to visitors, local restaurants, and food stores. The monastery produces nine award-winning cheeses, including Fontina fumé, Le Moine, and Bleu Bénédictin, with options that are gluten-free and lactose-free. They also maintain orchards with 3,500 apple trees and produce six varieties of apple cider, such as brut, demi-sec, and kir abbatial. If I had been allowed to bring food back to the UK, I would have purchased a box of six cheeses.

I left the boutique and went upstairs to find Fr. Blanche, with whom I had corresponded before starting my trip. Hearing a voice, I followed it to the porter's lodge, where a monk was on the phone behind a glass window. Our eyes met, and he stepped out of his office to greet me.

"Fr. Blanche, I presume?" I spoke.

"Yes, how can I help you?" he replied.

I asked if they had any rooms available for the next two days where I could work, but he explained that all rooms were occupied by a conference of 50 people. He had mentioned this to me months earlier, but I had been so eager that I thought I might still find a way. I was wrong. I then asked if they had any quiet spaces, like a library or a desk with Wi-Fi, but they didn't. The monastery is a place of quiet reflection, not work. I felt a little disappointed, as I had hoped to work in such a peaceful environment. Still, there was no blame or shame—just acceptance.

My room at Dans Les Bras de Memphré was perfectly pleasant. I imagined it as a private cottage near the abbey, and I continued my journaling there. The universe, it seemed, had my back. On the day of my departure, I mentioned to Ghislaine that over the past three days, my room—with its two large windows overlooking her gardens—had felt like a sanctuary. She smiled and told me that when they had bought the property years ago, it was called Le Relais de L'Abbaye, meaning "The Inn at the Abbey." Serendipitously, this was exactly what I had been looking for, even more so than a spartan room at the monastery. All's well that ends well.

On Saturday, I spent most of the day summarizing significant and insightful moments from each country I had visited over the past 80 days. I took a break to visit Lake Magog at Georgeville, which was stunningly beautiful. For lunch, I went to Atessa, an upscale Italian restaurant on Magog's main street. I ordered a salad, the pasta of the day, a non-alcoholic Heineken, and finished with a vanilla ice cream affogato. Afterward, I walked to the supermarket to buy food for dinner.

When I returned to my car, I found a parking ticket under the windshield. I refused to let it upset me.

I spent the rest of the day in my room, journaling, reading, and watching television. Dinner at six consisted of cheese, grapes, biscuits, and fresh raspberries I had bought earlier from the supermarket.

On Sunday morning, I woke up at 6:30 a.m. Ghislaine prepared breakfast for me at 7:30, and by 9:00 a.m., I was in my car heading to Le Spa Manoir Hovey in North Hatley, about 20 minutes away. I had booked a one-hour massage to release all the tension in my body, followed by a final gourmet meal before my three-hour drive to Montreal International Airport. There, I dropped off my car at the Avis/Budget rental office and walked to the terminal to catch my British Airways flight BA94 to London Heathrow.

I landed at Heathrow Airport at 9:50 a.m. local time on Monday, June 10th, having completed my "Around the World in Eighty Days" tour.

CONCLUSION

"Life is an unfoldment, and the further we travel, the more truth we can comprehend."

Hypatia (350-415 AD)
An Alexandrian woman, philosopher,
astronomer, and mathematician

My travels around the world in eighty days were an enjoyable, educational, and enriching experience. Upon my return, I spent several months decompressing, deconstructing, and developing on the epiphanies and revelations I had encountered. These insights, I hope, will not only guide me but also inspire you in the next chapters of our life journeys.

After compiling all my notes, I organized my experiences under three main themes:

1. What can nature teach us?
2. How can suffering and sacrifice transform us?
3. Why does changing our mindset also change our lives?

1. What can nature teach us?

Albert Einstein once shared profound insights about nature, saying, "Look deep into nature, and then you will understand everything better," and "If you want to understand the Universe, just look at nature." He also remarked, "We still do not know one thousandth of one percent of what nature has revealed to us."

I witnessed the truth of these words during my five-day safari at Rockfig Lodge in the Timbavati Private Nature Reserve, nestled in the northwest of Kruger National Park, South Africa, near the border with Mozambique.

One day, I observed a lion lazily feasting on its fresh kill—a wildebeest—all by itself. I learned that a lion's life is a cycle of feast or famine. Hunting requires immense energy, so lions target larger prey like giraffes, zebras, and wildebeests. After a successful hunt, a lion eats for three days and sleeps up to 20 hours a day to digest its meal. On another occasion, I watched a lioness hunt at dusk to feed her three cubs. The cubs, eager to join her, were met with a stern look from their mother, which sent them whimpering back to safety. Life for lions is fraught with risk; a single kick from a giraffe or zebra can break a lion's jaw, leading to a slow death by thirst or starvation.

One particularly hot afternoon, as I relaxed by the lodge pool with a drink, I witnessed a majestic parade of elephants approaching. Guests and staff alike watched in silent reverence. I later discovered that the lodge owner had built a watering hole just below the pool to attract elephants and other animals for our viewing pleasure. About 15 elephants approached—a large matriarch, several males, and many females with their calves. The matriarch shooed away some younger males for their unruly behavior. The sense of family devotion and emotion among the elephants was palpable, leaving a lasting impression on me.

I also had the delightful opportunity to observe the elegance of the leopard. If the lion is the king of the jungle, the leopard must be its emperor. It's no wonder Zulu kings wear leopard skins to symbolize power and nobility. While lions live in communities in open country, leopards are solitary creatures, dwelling deeper in nature and making them far more elusive. A lion's plain coat pales in comparison to the leopard's stunning, patterned fur, which not only adds to its beauty but also serves as effective camouflage during hunts and against predators.

Early one morning, we spotted a baby grey duiker, a small antelope, standing lost on the road. Our driver guessed its mother had likely become dinner the night before. Naively, I asked if we could take it back to the lodge. He replied that if they followed that logic, the lodge would have become a zoo by now. Nature is both beautiful and brutal, and whether we like it or not, it must take its course. The baby duiker would likely become lunch or dinner by sunset. How often do we interfere with the natural order out of sentimentality? And do we ever question the wisdom of such actions?

Nature's brutality is starkly evident in the hunting methods of African wild dogs. When they target a solitary impala or antelope, they tear it apart, one bite at a time. These dogs are not only terrifyingly efficient hunters but also striking in their physical appearance and demeanor. Yet, they, too, are part of nature's design.

Whether in South Africa's Timbavati Game Reserve or Australia's Whitsunday Islands, the sunrises and sunsets are breathtaking. They remind us to treat each day as a lifetime—to relish every moment and not squander the present, for it is all we truly have. The past is gone, and the future is uncertain.

In Kaikoura, on New Zealand's South Island, I spent half a day swimming with dolphins. I learned that dolphins lead a promiscuous lifestyle. A female may mate with up to five males (paternity is never an issue for this species!) and then, alongside other pregnant dolphins, form a creche during her 11-month pregnancy. They nurture their young for up to two years, teaching them to hunt before returning to the dating scene. This cycle repeats six or seven times over their 20-year lifespan. Would you believe that polyandry - where a woman takes two or more husbands - is practiced in some tribes in North India, Nepal, Tibet, and some Massai tribes in Kenya? They do so not only for economic survival reasons but also to keep the cohesion in the larger family units.

Water is another element we often take for granted. It makes up 75 percent of our bodies and is essential for survival. Being mindful of water—its importance, its feel on our skin, its physical and spiritual properties of purification—can elevate our minds and spirits. I noticed that New Zealand, Japan, and Canada all have an abundance of water. Without a doubt, water is the new oil in terms of natural resources.

One of my most memorable experiences was on a beach in New Zealand's Coromandel Peninsula, near Hahei. The beach is famous for its natural hot water pools, where visitors dig into the sand to create their own warm baths. The minerals in the water leave you feeling rejuvenated. Later, the tide comes in, washing away the pools and resetting the beach for another day.

In Japan, every village and town seem to have streams of water running through it. The *onsens*, or hot springs, were a daily highlight for me. In Canada, the lakes, rivers, and waterfalls are a feast for the eyes and soul. The majestic snow-capped Canadian Rockies and endless forests made the three-hour journey along the Icefields Parkway (Highway 93)—the most spectacular highway in the world—an unforgettable experience. Quebec City, I discovered, is a natural fortress, strategically controlling the waterways in and out of North America. This is why the British, French, and Americans fought so fiercely over it.

2. How can suffering and sacrifice transform us?

Khalil Gibran, the Lebanese American poet, once wrote, "Out of suffering have emerged the strongest souls; the most massive characters are seared with scars."

One of the reasons I visited Robben Island, near Cape Town, was to witness the environment that transformed Nelson Mandela from a fiery revolutionary into a humble leader. Why is this important? Because in retirement, many of us expect life to become blissful, only to find it isn't. Instead, retirement offers an opportunity to remake ourselves into the person we might have wanted to be earlier in life but were prevented from becoming. It's a chance to do what we love before the lights go out. The journey after retirement is a new beginning, and all new beginnings are painful. Yet, if we have the courage to endure, we can emerge stronger and more loving.

Elisabeth Kübler-Ross wrote, "The most beautiful people we have known are those who have known defeat, known suffering, known struggle, known loss, and have found their way out of those depths."

The French Huguenots are a testament to this. They were French Protestants who fled to South Africa in the late 1600s and early 1700s to escape religious persecution in France. The Dutch East India Company encouraged them to settle at the Cape of Good Hope to strengthen the agricultural base and support a Dutch supply station and trading post. By 1692, around 300 Huguenots had settled in the valley and town of Franschhoek, meaning "French Corner." Today, Franschhoek boasts some of the finest residential homes and restaurants in the country, along with 45 vineyards covering 50 square miles. Tourists can explore these vineyards using the hop-on, hop-off wine trams. This beautiful corner of South Africa was born from the suffering and sacrifice of the Huguenots.

Between 1919 and 1932, Australia's returned soldiers built the Great Ocean Road, a 240-kilometer stretch along the southeastern coast near Melbourne, between Torquay and Allansford. Dedicated to soldiers killed during World War I, it is the world's largest war memorial. The road winds through diverse terrain, including rainforests, beaches, and cliffs made of limestone and sandstone, which are prone to erosion. It provides access to iconic landmarks like the Twelve Apostles limestone stacks (now reduced to eight due to erosion). In 2008, the Royal Automobile Club of Victoria (RACV) named it the state's top tourism experience. Once again, beauty emerged from suffering and sacrifice, creating something that benefits us all.

Similarly, in New Zealand, public works such as road and rail networks created jobs and progress for the young nation. The country boasts 29 road tunnels and 150 rail tunnels spanning over 87 kilometers. Its mountainous terrain made railway construction particularly challenging, necessitating tunnels to traverse hills and mountains. One of the most notable is the Otira Tunnel, a railway tunnel in the South Island that runs under the Southern Alps from Arthur's Pass to Otira, stretching over 8.5 kilometers. The gradient is steep, with the Otira end over 250 meters lower than the Arthur's Pass end. Construction began in 1907, and the tunnel opened in 1923, taking 16 years to complete. At the time, it was the seventh-longest tunnel in the world. This achievement underscores that nothing great is accomplished without suffering. To survive and thrive, humans must find meaning in their suffering.

In Japanese culture, I observed that suffering is not just a part of life—it *is* life. It is through suffering that one develops expertise and mastery in any pursuit. Suffering is not to be avoided but embraced. It is not an ugly word in Japan; rather, it is intertwined with discipline. Despite the transformative Meiji Restoration of 1868 and the post-World War II rebuilding in 1945, Japanese culture remains deeply rooted in the Samurai ethos of service above self, devotion to discipline, sacrifice, and resilience.

During World War II, Japan's resilience and persistence were on full display. Even after losing the war, the Japanese refused to surrender. They launched *kamikaze* missions, where pilots flew planes into enemy warships, causing maximum damage. Another secret *kamikaze* mission, based in Hiroshima, involved teenagers willing to die for their country. Their goal was to pilot small boats loaded with explosives into US warships. The atomic bomb dropped on Hiroshima ended this mission before it could be carried out.

The word "Hiroshima" is inextricably linked with suffering. The scale of carnage is incomprehensible: 80,000 people were incinerated instantly, and another 60,000 suffered from illnesses for years or decades. The horrors included severe burns, blisters, and skin hanging from bodies like rags. The personal stories of men, women, and children were harrowing. Yet, the spirit of Hiroshima moved me deeply. The survivors' message was clear: "No one else should suffer as we have."

I think of retirees who have drifted into the oblivion of dementia because they stopped living. What a tragic loss—to themselves, their families, and humanity. I came to Hiroshima to see how a city reduced to ashes could rebuild itself. I wanted to draw inspiration from Hiroshima's journey from disaster to renewal—a space I call the "liminal space" or "cloud of unknowing"—as a model for retirees navigating their own transitions.

The *hibakusha* (survivors of the atomic bomb) emerged from a cauldron of suffering with a message that transcends hatred and rejection. Their spirit of generosity and love for humanity offers a profound focus on the future of humankind.

3. Why does changing our mindset also change our lives?

Our mindset is the combination of our conscious mind (the thinking or rational mind) and our subconscious mind (the emotional or intuitive mind). Albert Einstein once wrote, "The intuitive mind is a sacred gift, and the rational mind is a faithful servant. We have created a society that honors the servant and has forgotten the gift." If we want to change our mindset, we cannot rely solely on the rational mind to solve the problem, as it will invariably fail us. Consider this: how many New Year's resolutions have you made that succeeded? If you want to change your mindset, you must focus on the intuitive mind.

Our mindset is deliberately limited because we seek to control the world around us. This is how our ego believes it can ensure our security, but this is a false sense of safety. The world is vast, and we can only perceive what our senses allow. No matter how intelligent or studious we are, we can only grasp an insignificantly small fraction of what is happening around us. During my safari in the Timbavati, I realized that my brain was wired very differently from my guide, Lorence, and tracker, Fumani. They could spot animals hidden in the bush from a distance, while I couldn't see them even up close. Fumani could find chameleons with a torch at night, while I only noticed them when we were within a foot.

Joseph Campbell, the American mythologist, once wrote, "The cave you fear to enter holds the treasure you seek." I used to think this "cave" was something external. Now, I realize it is our own skull. This understanding led me to see that what differentiates us all is the wiring of our neurons and synapses. The good news is that, with practice, we can rewire our brains as easily as a spider weaves a new web. We can create a new inner dialogue to replace the old one. For example, your current inner dialogue might say, "I'm too old to learn public speaking." Your new inner dialogue could say, "I'm excited to join Toastmasters, learn to speak in public, and make new friends on the same journey." With 20 or more years ahead of us, we must renew our mindset to seize the opportunities life offers.

The act of walking creates not just external motion but internal transformation. During my travels, I did a great deal of walking and hiking on challenging terrains, each with its own difficulties. On the Roberg Peninsula in South Africa, the challenge was navigating rocks and stones. On Hamilton Island in Australia, it was walking on pebbles and sand. In Abel Tasman National Park in New Zealand, steep inclines and precarious paths tested me. On the Nakasendo Trail in Nagiso, Japan, debris on the pathways made the journey tricky. And in the Rocky Mountains of Alberta, Canada, the challenge was not getting lost while exploring the idyllic lakes. Yet, these walks gave me the opportunity for an "inventure"—an adventure within.

It dawned on me that Christian pilgrimages, such as the Camino de Santiago (The Way of St. James), which began in the 9th century and continues today, offer a similar opportunity for inner exploration. Each year, around 300,000 people walk 800 kilometers (500 miles) from San Sebastian in southern France, along the northern coastline of Spain, to Santiago on the Atlantic Ocean. Walking through long and difficult terrain, meeting strangers along the way, and staying overnight in hostels provides the time and space needed to discover what we desire in the next chapter of our lives.

In the past, traveling with someone always appealed to me, not just for the romantic aspect but also for having someone to share thoughts with. If I traveled alone, I would often envy couples who were together. Fast forward to the present, and I no longer felt that way on this trip. I could wake up early and start my day without worrying about adjusting my plans for a partner. (This is not a critique of partnerships.) The entire day was mine to do as I pleased. If I didn't feel like doing something, I simply didn't do it. Over time, I realized that I loved my own company.

Traveling solo was a beautiful experience, and I met wonderful people along the way. I could be myself—my playful self, my thoughtful self. I didn't have to worry about including a partner in conversations or avoiding people they might not enjoy, even if I wanted to engage with them. I didn't feel lonely at all. In fact, I cherished the solitary time I had to myself. It was a treat!

Being solitary also allows us to become observers of human behavior. I recall watching a mother chastise her adolescent son in public for being selfish and wanting to do what he wanted, while she had to tend to her hospitalized mother. I felt the pain of both the mother and her son, as I've been in both situations at different times in my life. Observing how others behave gives us a glimpse into our own actions and makes us more compassionate—not just toward others, but also toward ourselves.

In my solo travels, I encountered many beautiful people—both outwardly and inwardly. I noticed stunning women in every country I visited, but I was particularly drawn to Japanese women. Their tendency to avoid direct eye contact made them seem mysterious and intriguing. When men are drawn to women, they often project imagined qualities onto them, qualities that are statistically unlikely to exist. I've been guilty of this myself. I've also met women who may not be conventionally beautiful but possess such a radiant disposition that they become magnetic. Dr. Elisabeth Kübler-Ross captured this idea perfectly when she wrote: "The most beautiful people we have known are those who have known defeat, known suffering, known struggle, known loss, and have found their way out of the depths. These persons have an appreciation, a sensitivity, and an understanding of life that fills them with compassion, gentleness, and a deep loving concern. Beautiful people do not just happen."

There is also beauty in the cultures I encountered. For example, I attended a Māori dance performance at the Auckland Museum. Before the performance, the head dancer explained that we should not applaud at the end of their dances. In Māori culture, applause is seen as unnecessary and even a form of control. Instead, if we enjoyed the performance, we could do a Māori wrist shake, a gesture that signifies resonance with what we experienced.

I also deeply appreciated the beauty of Japanese culture. I wholeheartedly agree with the sentiments of renowned chef Alain Ducasse, who said, "It is impossible to remain indifferent to Japanese culture. It is a different civilization where all you have learned must be forgotten. It is a great intellectual challenge and a gorgeous sensual experience." That was exactly my experience of Japan. I didn't compare it to my own culture or any other. Nor did I listen to those who criticized Japan as a racist country—I didn't experience that at all. Instead, I was struck by the politeness and discipline evident in every aspect of life, from hotels and restaurants to city streets and village paths. It's true that politeness, a cultural trait, doesn't necessarily mean someone is a good person, but who am I to judge? I can only reflect on how they made me feel: welcomed and respected.

I thoroughly enjoyed learning about Japan's history, culture, food, and religion. I was horrified by the devastation wrought on Hiroshima by the atomic bomb, yet I was deeply moved by the spirit of forgiveness and resilience displayed at the Hiroshima Peace Memorial Museum. I found Japan's history, particularly that of the Samurai, utterly captivating. However, I also recognized the dark side of an excessive love for culture and history: it can imprison our mindset. Like the British, the Japanese are often confined by their cultural mindset, which I believe can be dangerous. It creates a false sense of security and stifles growth.

In a world that is changing faster than ever, a fixed mindset is a recipe for disaster. We're told that the next 20 years will bring more change than the past 20, which were already unprecedented. If this is true—and I believe it is—then we need a growth mindset to navigate these uncharted waters.

My own mindset about religion and spirituality also evolved during my time in Japan. Instead of focusing on differences, I began to seek out similarities. I observed three key things. First, while spirituality is a deeply personal journey, religion is rooted in culture and community. Striking a balance between the two is essential. Too much religion, and you risk losing yourself; too much spirituality, and you risk losing connection with others. Second, I noticed the fervent devotion of worshippers at temples. It became clear to me that their faith, not the offerings they made to temple priests, was what would bring about the fulfillment of their desires. Third, I realized that cultures and religions are all grappling to understand what lies beyond the limits of time, space, and our sensory perception of God, the Universe, or the Source. As a result, humans have created diverse explanations for the inexplicable.

For example, Buddhists worship 1,000 gods, each representing a different challenge in life. Muslims use 99 adjectives to describe the power and majesty of God. Jews, out of respect and reverence, refrain from uttering God's name directly, referring to Him simply as Yahweh or "I am who I am." Christians believe in a triune God—Father, Son, and Holy Spirit—three persons in one. While these explanations are plausible, they all fall short because our understanding is inherently limited.

One of the most significant lessons I learned was the importance of identity and its impact on our mindset. Our name, or what we are called, shapes how others see us and how we see ourselves. It can either help us feel a sense of belonging or mark us as outsiders. Where we come from also leaves an indelible mark. For instance, if you belong to an immigrant community, you may feel different and possibly experience antipathy from others. Your language and accent can further set you apart, highlighting your differences from the community you live in.

What we wear also communicates who we are. Clothing does more than cover our bodies—it reveals our preferences, beliefs, aspirations, and even our socioeconomic status. Brand names, colors, textures, styles, and cosmetics all project an image, whether we intend them to or not. Similarly, what we eat does more than nourish us—it reflects our tastes, beliefs, and cultural heritage.

Lastly, the work we do says something about us to others, but more importantly, it reveals something to us about ourselves. If your work doesn't bring you joy, it's time to find work that does. Ask yourself these four questions: What am I good at? What do I love to do? What does the world need? What can

I be paid for? Who we are is just as important as our purpose or meaning in life. In the next chapter of our lives, we have the opportunity to reinvent ourselves.

Our identity is not set in stone, nor are our values and beliefs. Our essence is far greater than our personality. We need to ask ourselves: Who do I want to be? What is the highest version of myself I can become? What new values and beliefs will guide me? Time is precious. Today is all we have, as no one is guaranteed tomorrow. So, what are you waiting for? Seize the moment!

ACKNOWLEDGMENTS

First, I would like to thank the team of country specialists at Audley Travel in Oxfordshire, particularly Ian Ross, Andy Freeman, and Alice Wright, for their invaluable support in planning this journey, as well as everyone at Caxton, the travel and multi-currency card, which helped me to pay for everything seamlessly on my world travels.

In South Africa, I extend my gratitude to my business partners, Christi Franken and Johan Van Zyl, who shared their Cape Town with me, including a memorable rugby match. I am also thankful to Bill and Jeri Russell for a delightful lunch on the waterfront. A special thanks to Vuliani, a guide, former political prisoner, and gracious human being, for sharing his painful yet inspiring experiences from his time incarcerated on Robben Island. At Rockfig Lodge in the Timbavati Nature Reserve, I am deeply grateful to the entire team—Liam, Mags, Nicole, Karel, Lorence, and Fumani—for their warmth and expertise.

In Sydney, Australia, my appreciation goes to Angela Galloway and Alexandra Andrews, friends from Modern Elder Academy in Baja, Mexico, for a wonderful lunch at Iceberg in Bondi Beach. I am grateful to Stephen Digby, a business acquaintance of 20 years from London, for a catch-up breakfast and reconnection. In Melbourne, I thank Stephen Huppert for our insightful breakfast meeting and discussions.

In Auckland, New Zealand, I thank Mike and Izzy Silverman, Toastmaster friends from my time in London, for their hospitality. I am also deeply grateful to Karel Wallace, owner of Cambria House in Nelson, and Skip Gregory, owner of The Factory in Kaikoura, for providing such personalized lodging and meals. Special thanks to Anna Harper for a delightful Thai dinner and her captivating storytelling. Lastly, I am thankful for the serendipitous encounters with Graham and Jenni McDougall of Queenstown, South Island, who became new friends.

In Japan, I offer gratitude to Raquel Spring for introducing me to her friend and shaman, Altair Shyam (Steven), with whom I enjoyed a memorable lunch. I extend my thanks to all my guides throughout Japan: Keiichi Tamura (Kei) in Tokyo, Ms. Kazu Takatsuka in Kanazawa, Hanai in Osaka, Inati in Miyajima, and Akio Miyashi and Akira Ishida in Kyoto. A special acknowledgment goes to the monks at Ekoin Monastery on Mount Koya and to my Samurai friend, Masahisa Shijiyami (Masa), in Kanazawa. I am also thankful for the new friendships formed with Lukas and Barbara Gresch from Bern, Switzerland, and Keith and Merrilyn from Perth, Australia.

In Vancouver, Canada, I thank Brian Spanier for leading our bicycle tour through Stanley Park, and Tammy Vigue, a fellow coach and mentor to retirees, for sharing her stories over brunch. My gratitude also goes to Paul Burrows, whose expertise as a historian and storyteller brought Quebec City to life for me. Lastly, I am thankful to Ghislaine and Michel, the owners of a serene sanctuary on Lake Memphremagog, not far from the Vermont border, for their hospitality and warmth.

A huge thanks for the team at Hasmark International Publishing, in Toronto, Canada, which includes Judy O'Beirn, Jenn Gibson, Ana-Maria Janes, Anne Karklins, book designer, and Brad Green, my editor, Allison Burney, my proofreader, for transforming my manuscript into this finished product.

Last but not least, I'm also grateful to my personal team: Jayne Cherrington-Cook for the social media posts, Deborah Carr for the book landing pages and my website, and James Wilson for the six maps.

ABOUT THE AUTHOR

GEORGE JERJIAN is a mindset mentor, author, and speaker who retired after being given six months to live by his oncologist. Thankfully, the diagnosis was wrong, and as soon as he could, he "unretired" and set to work helping his tribe of baby boomers do the same.

George holds a business degree from Bradford University Management Centre in England and a master's degree in journalism from New York University. With over 40 years of business experience, he has worked as a Chartered Marketer, a partner in a US commercial real estate venture, and a financial advisor.

An Emmy Award-winning producer, Distinguished Toastmaster, and author of 12 books, George's most recent works—*Spirit of Gratitude*, *DARE to Discover Your Purpose*, and *Odyssey of an Elder*—form a trilogy focused on creating a new beginning after retirement.

© **George Jerjian 2025**

ADVANCE PRAISE

Odyssey of an Elder shows us the benefits of taking a gap year after retirement to discern our evolving identity and attune to our new purpose.

—KEN DYCHTWALD PhD,
psychologist/gerontologist/author,
founder & CEO of Age Wave, USA

George's Odyssey shows that curiosity doesn't retire – and neither should adventure.

—RUPERT LEE-BROWNE,
CEO of Caxton (the travel money card), UK

I've always believed that life is meant to be *lived fully*—not just endured—and George Jerjian is living proof of what's possible when we choose growth, reinvention, and deep inner alignment, no matter our age or stage of life. In *Odyssey of an Elder*, George takes us on a powerful and personal journey—around the world, yes—but also deep into the soul. His story is rich with wisdom, courage, and the kind of raw honesty that wakes you up and makes you reflect on your own life. After a brush with mortality, a divorce, and a powerful reckoning with what it really means to live *on purpose*, George doesn't just talk about transformation—he lives it. This is more than a travel memoir. It's a call to live boldly, to question the scripts we've been handed, and to step fully into the life we're meant to lead. Whether you're navigating transition, seeking clarity, or simply craving inspiration—this book is a gift.

—Dr. PEGGY McCOLL,
New York Times Bestselling Author, Canada

Reading *Odyssey of an Elder* felt like travelling with an old friend—one who's not afraid to ask big questions and laugh at himself along the way. Jerjian's story is both deeply personal and universally relatable. It made me want to pack a bag, board a plane, and start living with more intention.

—ANDREW KING, world traveller, vacation consultant, and author of the Visual Journey Series, Canada

As a therapist, I found this journey *Odyssey of an Elder* to be more than just travel - it's a moving exploration of resilience, wonder, and self-discovery. A reminder that the most meaningful journeys often take us inward. A beautiful read.

—HELEN MARIE SANDLE,
psychotherapist, author of *Choose You*,
and podcast host for *I don't think we talk enough about…*, UK

Odyssey of an Elder is a joyful, honest, and sometimes mischievous reminder that retirement isn't the end of the road. Along the way, Jerjian sheds old layers and picks up new perspective—showing us that travel can be a teacher, a therapist, and a thrill ride all at once. If you've ever dreamed of hopping the next flight out, this book gives you the map *and* the motivation.

—WES MOSS, author of *What the Happiest Retirees Know* and Host of *Retire Sooner* podcast, USA

In *Odyssey of An Elder: Around the World in Eighty Days*, George Jerjian shares his remarkable story of how a terminal misdiagnosis at 52 became the catalyst for profound personal transformation. What followed was a bold unraveling—leaving a relationship, traveling to five countries, and reimagining the shape of his life. George's journey is an invitation for any middlescent seeking growth, perspective, and the courage to embrace their next chapter. He reminds us that it's never too late to live a life of intention and possibility."

—BARBARA WAXMAN,
gerontologist, coach, longevity advocate, and speaker, USA

Odyssey of an Elder is a reflective, engaging read that reinforces the idea that childhood dreams can come true at any age and that travel offers essential elements to a meaningful life including awe, gratitude, relationships, and well-being.

—ROBERT LAURA,
founder of The Retirement Coaches Association, USA

Odyssey of an Elder is more than a travel memoir—it's a profound journey of self-discovery, reinvention, and spiritual awakening. After decades of work and a painful divorce, mindset mentor George Jerjian chooses to walk his talk, embarking on an 80-day adventure across five continents. What unfolds is a deeply personal narrative that challenges our perceptions of aging, purpose, and the power of embracing life's second act with curiosity and courage. With humor, heart, and unflinching honesty, George invites us to reflect on our own paths: What are we leaving behind, and what are we moving toward? For those navigating retirement or life's transitions, this book is both a mirror and a map—an inspiring testament that it's never too late to explore the world or rediscover yourself. As a retirement coach, I found George's story not only affirming but transformational. I had the pleasure of meeting him when his journey brought him to Vancouver, and his presence was every bit as insightful as his words. His message is clear: life after retirement isn't an ending—it's an odyssey waiting to begin.

—TAMMY VIGUE, Retirement coach, Canada

Jules Verne created a genre called *voyages extraordinaires*. George adds to this with his book that unfolds both as a travel guide and a later life guide. Pack your bags, fasten your seat belt, and question not where are you going but who are you.

—DAMIAN STANCOMBE, CEO
of 60 Paydays to Retirement, UK

Odyssey of an Elder addresses the worthy topics of purpose, reinvention and the challenges of retirement based on the real-life experiences of mindset coach George Jerjian as he travels across five countries in 80 days. Both inspiring and practical - a great read for adventurous souls embarking on their retirement journey.

—SUSAN LATREMOILLE, CPRC,
author, keynote speaker,
co-founder Next Chapter Lifestyle Advisors, Canada

Through fascinating stories from his 80-day journey of self-discovery to five countries he had never visited, the book concludes with three main themes he found to be both "epiphanies and revelations." A truly inspiring read to guide the next chapter of your life journey!

—REID STONE,
founder of My Life's Encore and
creator of the MLE Longevity Network, US

A captivating journey through retirement and renewal, where global travels reveal nature's splendour and the transformative power of identity.

—STEPHEN HUPPERT,
consultant and advisor, focused on improving retirement outcomes, Australia

From the very first page, I felt like I was sitting right next to George in every country he visited! What I love most about George's book is how honest he is about his feelings. This book isn't just a travel story - it's like having a super wise friend show you that even when life gets hard, you can still find joy again. It makes me braver about my own life too!

—KATHY TAROCHIONE,
founder & CEO, The Golden Life Community LLC, *a lifestyle empowerment organization for mature women*, USA

George Jerjian's *Odyssey of an Elder* is a moving and powerful reminder that life's greatest adventures often begin when we dare to let go of what no longer serves us. Through his bold, honest, and deeply personal journey, George shows us that growth, wonder, and renewal are possible at any stage of life. His story is an inspiring call to live with curiosity, courage, and heart—proving that the best chapters are often still ahead.

—MARC MICHAELSON, coach, author,
Leadership Development Innovator, and Workplace Culture Shaper @ Work Designed for Thriving, USA

On so many levels, undertaking such a monumental journey is not for the faint hearted. Whilst it is George's personal odyssey and owning his elderhood, there are lessons to be learned in his sharing and the poignant questions he asks. What childhood dream might we have forsaken, which we could reignite to enrich, enlighten, and empower us in our next chapter?

>   —ANNE HARPER, guide and advisor, Certified Narrative Coach, and founder of The Tall Journey, New Zealand

George Jerjian's *Odyssey of an Elder* is more than a travel memoir—it's a bold invitation to shed old identities and step into a life of renewed purpose. With raw honesty and soulful insight, George shows us that it's never too late to grow, grieve, and begin again. A powerful reminder that the real journey is always within.

>   —JAMES SCOTT-WONG, author of the International Bestselling Series: *The Adventures of Pierre and Penny LePockets: Pierre's Promise of the Deep*, UK

Have you ever wanted to travel and fully experience the world? In this book, George engages us in each aspect of his journey. With him, I experienced the places, the views, the feelings, the foods, the wines, the cultures, and most importantly, the insights he gained. This is such a transparent sharing of a life-changing adventure.

>   —MICHELLE FRITSCH, PharmD, BCGP, co-founder, of Propel Comprehensive Wellness and Life Purpose Scan, USA

Join George Jerjian on his journey around the world (great stories), into his new life in elderhood (insightful) and his personal growth (invaluable). He learned a lot and there is a lot for you to learn from him while enjoying the journey.

>   —PAUL LONG,
>   founder, New Way Forward, USA

From conversations with local chefs to encounters off the beaten path, this book invites you to savor life in all its flavors. A beautiful reminder that the best journeys begin with saying yes to yourself.

—JAE M. RANG, author: 50 Simple Ways to Release the Shackles of Self-Sabotage, Canada

Beautifully written, brave, and unexpectedly funny. George's reflections on change, loss, and the power of movement stayed with me long after the last page. A book for anyone curious about the world—and about themselves. Highly recommended!

—JUDY O'BEIRN,
President and CEO of Hasmark Publishing, Canada

SALES PAGE

Other books available on all Amazon sites:
Spirit of Gratitude: Crises are Opportunities
DARE to Discover Your Purpose: Retire/Refire/Rewire

- Website link - www.georgejerjian.com
- Email address - george@georgejerjian.com

- Social media networks/handles:

Facebook - @retirementrebellion
Instagram - @retirementrebellion
YouTube - @retirementrebellion
Linkedin - @georgejerjian
X - @georgejerjian

www.ingramcontent.com/pod-product-compliance
Ingram Content Group UK Ltd.
Pitfield, Milton Keynes, MK11 3LW, UK
UKHW020630100725
6821UKWH00019B/712